OGHENETHOJA UMUTEME

The Man
God Made

Understand the qualities expected of those who
live life to its fullest and make heaven at the end of the day

MEMOIRS

Cirencester

The Man God Made

Published by Memoirs

MEMOIRS
PUBLISHING

Memoirs Books

25 Market Place, Cirencester, Gloucestershire, GL7 2NX
info@memoirsbooks.co.uk www.memoirspublishing.com

Address all enquiries to the publisher,
Restoration Media House Limited +234-8092496045, +2348076190064
Email: rmhltd.info@gmail.com

Printed in England

The Man God Made

CONTENTS

DEDICATION

PROLOGUE

DEDICATION

To everyone called by God to restore mankind back to Him; through the teaching of the gospel of Jesus Christ, and making the world to see, the Lord Jesus, crucified for their sins.

PROLOGUE

This book was inspired by the Holy Spirit at about 5am on the 11th day of November 2011, with the message that the Lord was looking for someone He could call His own. He is looking for anyone who will take up the mantle of leadership and deliverance, who will only say what God says, and go where God sends them. He is in search of any man who has the seed of the Lamb of God in his heart.

Whenever the Earth experiences chaos, God intervenes. Right from the beginning of creation, He has never stopped rescuing the world from calamities caused by man's insatiable quest. The Man God Made is the man whom God uses as an instrument of restoration.

In Isaiah 42:22, God raised a concern that no one could restore His creation to the order it was in when He made it, for His pleasure. God found Noah at a time when the world was soaked in human atrocities, yet Noah ended up cursing his grandson, and that singular act shows that he was unqualified as the Man God Made. Someone on a rescue mission would not lay a curse on those he was trying to rescue.

Abraham came to the scene, but his lie about his wife also disqualified him. Moses was up and working for God, but for lack of self control he was disqualified by God from restoring the land of Canaan back to his children. God was pleased with Job, but during Job's travail we could see that he had not indoctrinated his family on how to fear God, as his wife wanted him to curse God and die.

David was a man after God's heart, but his disqualification would be seen when God rejected him as one who would build his temple. Solomon ruled with the wisdom of God, but he was led astray to serve other gods by his wives, and that was where his disapproval from God came. If not for Christ's sake, Peter's denial of ever knowing Christ would have received a death blow as happened to Moses, yet Peter died crucified upside down. Who then is qualified to be God's approved man?

This is the reason we are in this discussion. God is looking for someone He would call His own, who will have the spirit of Christ crying in their hearts. The disciples of Jesus once asked: "Who then can be saved?" (Matthew 19:25). When Jesus revealed the secret that would lead to man's restoration, they replied: "This is a hard saying; who can understand it?" (John 6:60).

The purpose of this book is to enable us to understand the qualities expected of those who would live life to its fullest and reach Heaven at the end of the day. These qualities will enable them to minister Christ to the world, wherever they may be, so that multitudes of souls may be saved from everlasting death in hell.

This book aims to bring the best out of everyone who will return to God for His leadership. As you read through it, write out those qualities you feel you may have been lacking. Then draw up a plan to address them with the facts presented in this book and see the improvement you will be getting in your day-to-day living, in your relationship with God, your career, marriage, business activities and overall thinking.

When this book is used as a family devotional, action tasks and targets can be drawn up for each member of the family to address, and reports can be fed back on progress made during the next devotional. This book can also be used as Sunday school material with the overall goal of developing a God-fearing personality in us. We could also use it as a training manual for pastors and other workers in the vineyard, so that they will become more useful to God.

In all, it is my belief that this book will definitely bring out the best in you. Happy studying.

Oghenethoja Umuteme
Founding President/Senior Pastor,
Royal Diamonds International Church
(Christ Movement International Ministries)
Port Harcourt, Nigeria

CHAPTER ONE

THE SEARCH IS ON

One might ask: "why is God interested in us?" The reason is not hard to find. He has created much wealth, and wants those who have His kind of heart to oversee this wealth. He is searching, looking into every nook and cranny – searching through the dark, deep down into the heart of man, ever searching for a flicker of any godly attribute in them, so that He can lead them into the path of spiritual awareness and they can walk with Him: *And when He finds one, He calls, and persuades them with promises. He would say "you are the head and not the tail, the blessings shall overtake you, I will make darkness light before you", and so on. These promises He also vows to fulfil if man would indeed turn back to Him: "These things will I do unto them, and not forsake them" – Isaiah 42:16.*

Yet not long after He had accepted those who returned into His Kingdom and revealed the secrets about Himself, His hidden treasures and the secret wisdoms in the Kingdom, He was disappointed. His new friends soon find solace in the arms of his age-long enemy the devil, who comes around, winking an eyebrow before God, in order to mock Him the more. And

God's beloved new friends abandon Him and follow His enemy to travel through the sea of pleasure and worldly treasures. There and then, God sits down, waiting patiently for His Spirit to woo another to Him, who will inherit His large kingdom with a song.

While the search is going on, the Angels are singing, but God refuses to be moved by their songs. The usual smile in His face has disappeared. His heart sings a song as He looks through the heart of men:

> *Love me, if you can -*
> *You are the one I love;*
> *Don't you run away from me,*
> *I am still waiting for you.*

The Angels had employed all manner of musical instruments both seen and unseen, if only God could turn to them and smile, but they failed; nothing pleased Him. The "Will" had been written from the foundation of the Earth. Every one of His sons who is in the Will had gone after his age-long enemy, the devil. He is a loving and caring father, and is not in a hurry to change the Will to suit what He now sees.

He sat there waiting for the next report of anyone who had turned away from His enemy. He overheard a shout of joy over a long distance. His heart beat for joy, hopeful of a harvest. Quickly He sent His Angels, with Archangel Gabriel leading the troupe.

When they got to Earth, they could not find "Faith" anywhere. The shout of joy that was overheard in Heaven was the shout of sports fans, those in club houses singing and dancing, political rallies and the like. Then the Angels burst into tears, singing:

He is waiting for you to grow
He is waiting for you to grow
He is waiting for you to grow
He is waiting for you to grow
Sometimes you cry, Sometimes you weep
It's not because God doesn't care
He is waiting for you to grow.

They sang this song all over the Earth, but none would listen. Meanwhile, Archangel Michael was still contending with the devil over the sons of God he held in bondage.

God was waiting for His Angels to return. They had gone all over the Earth in search for faith: none was found. And they continued with a new song:

I am your brother
I am your sister
You've gone away from home from so long a time
I've come to take you home.

3

Yet no one responded to the call to return to the Father. Then the Spirit of the Lord Himself left the throne of Heaven, proceeding from God, and He announced to God that a few people had been found who were willing to be trained and empowered.

The likes of Noah, Job and Abraham were found and used by God. Despite their shortcomings, God at least found "Faith." He called a new meeting, knowing that the devil, His age-long enemy, would stop at nothing in turning hearts away from Him, a fact He confirmed from the shortcomings of those that had turned to Him.

And because He found little faith through the lives of Noah, Job and Abraham, God proposed in His heart to rescue mankind. Looking to His right hand, there sat His only beloved and begotten son – the Lamb who is the foundation of all He ever laboured for. - John 1:1, Rev. 13:8.

The Angels brought ill reports from the Earth. The Lamb cried as He saw the tears from the eyes of God, His father, whose eyes were already running with streams of tears. This we know, that God cries too, because Jesus did weep over Lazarus (John 11:35) and Jerusalem (Luke 19:41-44). He only did what He saw God do in Heaven, which He confirmed in John 5:19: Jesus gave them this answer: *"Very truly I tell you, the Son can do nothing by himself; he can do only what he sees his Father doing, because whatever the Father does the Son also does.*

God is filled with emotion. Jesus also is filled with emotion. The Holy Spirit replicates this emotional character in whomever He possesses to do God's will. God looked at the Angels – one said the Earth should be destroyed, but God saw His rainbow and shook His head. He had regretted creating mankind, until He found Noah (Genesis 6:3, 5-6).

Archangel Michael wanted the devil bound forever, but God did not give in to that opinion because it wasn't time to bind the devil yet (Revelation 20:1-2). God looked again at Jesus and said, "The man I made must not perish." Jesus, who was right there with the father during the making of man, knew exactly what God was saying (John 1:1), because during the creation events the Angels were on guard and worshipping God, and as such they didn't have full details of what God had done to create the Earth and man. Jesus was the architect who designed all we see today, and He was fully in charge of both the creation and ensuring that everything was in perfect order.

The Angels, who are easily vexed by man's shortcomings (Exodus 23:20), would not be patient. To them, ending the world would limit their duties, and as such they could just be in Heaven ministering to God and eating manna (Psalm 78:24-25).

"What will become of the man I made?" God thought within Himself. Jesus knew what was in the heart of the Father, because He and the father are one (John 14:11). He smiled. He called on Angel Gabriel and commanded him to go and visit a young virgin with the message of redemption. God looked at Him. "You can't do that my son!" He said. "But Dad, you aren't happy," Jesus replied. God touched Jesus' face with His right palm, robbing softly, and then He kissed Him.

Also I heard the voice of the Lord, saying, Whom shall I send, and who will go for us? Then said I, Here am I; send me. - Isaiah 6:8

Jesus had His plan well mapped out:

1. *He will come in Human form and live with them: Let this mind be in you which was also in Christ Jesus, who, being in the form of God, did not consider it robbery to be equal with God, but made Himself of no reputation, taking the form of a bondservant, and coming in the likeness of men. And being found in appearance as a man, He humbled Himself and became obedient to the point of death, even the death of the cross. - Philippians 2:5-8.*

2. *He will take over their sins, so that God can lengthen their days, to allow them enough time to repent: The next day John saw Jesus coming toward him, and said, "Behold! The Lamb of God who takes away the sin of the world! - John 1:29*

3. *Since Judgment is in His hands, He will train them on what it takes to qualify as heirs of the Kingdom, exactly as God will want it done: For the Father judges no one, but has committed all judgment to the Son, that all should honour the Son just as*

they honour the Father. He who does not honour the Son does not honour the Father who sent Him. "Most assuredly, I say to you, he who hears My word and believes in Him who sent Me has everlasting life, and shall not come into judgment, but has passed from death into life. Most assuredly, I say to you, the hour is coming, and now is, when the dead will hear the voice of the Son of God; and those who hear will live. - John 5:22-25,

4. For the first time in the history of mankind, Man will experience what God does in Heaven. He will wake up with them and sleep with them. The entire Earth will become God's creative and healing workshop: Then Jesus answered and said to them, "Most assuredly, I say to you, the Son can do nothing of Himself, but what He sees the Father do; for whatever He does, the Son also does in like manner. For the Father loves the Son, and shows Him all things that He Himself does; and He will show Him greater works than these, that you may marvel. - John 5:19-20.

5. He will live by example, in his glory as it is in Heaven, in their midst: And the Word became flesh and dwelt among us, and we beheld His glory, the glory as of the only begotten of the Father, full of grace and truth. - John 1:14.

6. He will speak in two languages: Pure to His elect, and in parables to the world: The disciples came to him and asked,

"Why do you speak to the people in parables?" He replied, "Because the knowledge of the secrets of the kingdom of Heaven has been given to you, but not to them. - Matthew 13:10-11(NIV).

7. *He will physically restore health to many, and peace to all that will believe in Him: The thief does not come except to steal, and to kill, and to destroy. I have come that they may have life, and that they may have it more abundantly. - John 10:10.*

8. *Looking at the mansions in Heaven (John 14:2), with no one to live in them, He made up His mind to take up the task.*

And Jesus left Heaven to Earth on the final rescue mission, with the host of Heaven's Field Marshall, the one who proceeds from the father - The Holy Spirit. By this action, Mary became pregnant with a seed of salvation that will bruise the head of the serpent (Genesis 3:15).

The Field Marshall had gone ahead to form the baby that would become Jesus. Heaven was sad, and God vowed to be wherever His son was. He sent the Angels to be on guard, to protect the redeemer of the world and all that He had created, His only begotten son, from the reckless touch of His enemy – the devil.

Before then, John the Baptist had prepared the way (Mark 1:3-4). At Jesus' baptism, the Father couldn't wait to announce to the whole world that Jesus was His only begotten son, and as such, anyone who wanted to leave the devil should listen to Jesus (Mark 9:7). No sooner had He made this assertion than the Man He Made chose to work and walk in the dark. And the verdict was pronounced:

"And this is the condemnation, that the light has come into the world, and men loved darkness rather than light, because their deeds were evil" - John 3:19.

God searched through the heart of man, but he saw only a desperately manifested evil (Jeremiah 17:9-10). Jesus commenced the building of the Kingdom of God here on Earth.

He went after the unlearned men, who were already living as though they were cast out (Acts 4:13). These were the fishermen (Matthew 4:18) and those who were idle (Matthew 20). These represented the very worst, which is why today, those who are arrested by God and used by God are actually the worst in the society (Luke 7:47) – criminals, fornicators, dupers, thieves, harlots, etc. To Him, if these are won, the task of winning the world back to God will be reduced, as these sets of people will go into every nook and cranny to fish out God's children who are been cursed and deceived by the devil daily (Psalms 10:7-9).

When the world came to Him, He was already living out the plan in Heaven which the Father had agreed to. And the disciples couldn't help but ask Him to teach them how to pray (Luke 11:1). Nicodemus, on his own, also came to seek the wisdom from Heaven (John 3:1-2). So, the plan was working. He intensified this with healings and deliverances, and the multitude came (John 5, 6). God was happy, now, in Heaven. The miracles came in like a flood. Satan was brutally wounded, so he was condescendingly angry, disrespecting every good work of Christ here on Earth by deceiving many that He was using the power of Beelzebub, and ensuring that the Jewish authorities were blind to the prophecies that had revealed Christ earlier to them, which abound in the scriptures (Matthew 5:17, John 19:36).

Satan turned the heart of the elected of God against Him. The Pharisees couldn't see any more, because they were far from God, and the Sadducees were too sad to know that God was with them and as such they could not receive the spirit of the Man God Made. They saw the truth, but they couldn't believe that truth could still prevail. They never thought that someone more perfect than Abraham could exist on Earth. To them, Abraham was perfect, yet Abraham never attained the status of the Man God Made. Jesus displayed the attribute of what God expects in the Man God Made.

When He told them secrets that could help them achieve this perfect nature and order, they saw it as a "hard thing" (John 6:66). Speaking in tongues, for instance, confuses the devil, because he does not understand the language of God's spirit. He only understands the language of the Angels. The language in Heaven is not uniform but varies (Revelation 14:3), with hierarchy. Hence God also did it to mankind at the Tower of Babel (Genesis 11:7-8). The angels don't see what God does unless by special permission (Genesis 1:26). Only Jesus sees it, because God needs Jesus in order to lay the foundation of whatever decision He is about to carry out.

So, Jesus is God's wisdom while the Holy Spirit is the action of God. He achieved His plan, and left behind on Earth, the Field Marshall to help us overcome the challenges of life that had led us into imperfection, so that each one of us would become, the Man God Made. The search is on: *For all those things has mine hand made, and all those things have been, says the LORD: but to this man will I look, even to him that is poor and of a contrite spirit, and trembles at my word. - Isaiah 66:2.*

CHAPTER TWO

MAN MADE IN AFFLUENCE

All things are yours. This is what the Bible says in 1 Corinthians 3:22. These things include God's servants, the world, life, death, things present or things to come. God never restricted any of us in whatsoever we do, but He also expects that we show restraint and live a life that will honour Him.

The book of Genesis in the Bible opened with a world without form which existed in nothingness. Something was fascinating about what God was doing in Heaven. Reading from the book of Genesis, chapter 1 from verse 1 to verse 25, tells us something about the extent God went to to ensure that everything was in order so that we would have no reason to regret our stay here on Earth.

First the Holy Spirit, the Field Marshall of the hosts of Heaven, came down to Earth as instructed by God, the Commander-in-Chief of the hosts of Heaven, to bring life into the Earth.

Where is Jesus in all these? Jesus is creation (John 1:1), He is the foundation of the world (1 Corinthians 3:15), slain as a lamb to ensure that there exists a proper foundation for the Earth to flourish with life (Revelation 13:8). He is the Chief Judge of the Supreme Court of Heaven, the heavenly judiciary system. He is the law that sets the whole universe in place and order, which He came to fulfil in His first coming. He is the clue to the life that scientists have been experimenting about for ages and the cure to all the woes upon mankind.

The book of John 1:1 declares that without Him the Commander-in-Chief and the Field Marshall have no reason to exist. Without Him nothing is made – He is God Himself: the wisdom of God in action (1 Corinthians 1:24, 30). This in context means that without Christ there was no wisdom for creation to be possible. All that while, the Lamb was speaking from the foundation, ensuring that whatsoever will exist was in perfect order, and indeed they were, because the the Lamb Himself is the root of perfection (Revelation 13:8).

The Earth received spiritual illumination at the spoken word: "JESUS." Every chaos on Earth bowed down when the Commander-in-Chief pronounced the name JESUS! Because He is the light of the world, and so that light that came to be in Genesis 1:3 was nothing else but JESUS. With Jesus now on Earth, operating as the illuminative power of God, everything fell into its rightful order and place.

The reason for the creation events in Genesis 1:1-25 was that

God was about to put His feet on Earth for the purpose of fellowship, and He needed a governor who would only beautify whatsoever existed on Jesus, because the Earth is His footstool:

Thus says the LORD, The Heaven is my throne, and the Earth is my footstool: where is the house that ye build unto me? and where is the place of my rest? - Isaiah 66:1

This explains the fact that the Man who was about to be "made" by God must not build on any other foundation but the one laid from the foundation of the world – JESUS! This was the plan and the purpose of all the stress of creation that God went through in Genesis chapter one. So the Earth was filled with all the provisions of life that would enable the Man God Made to be in full control, and be able to do the will of the Commander-in-Chief, which is: ensuring that Jesus was confessed as the "existence of creation".

In creation week, the sea received the instruction of the Commander-in-Chief, and life multiplied within it and in the bowel of all the waters that flow into it. The Heavens did same, and the Earth also brought forth. There was total affluence on Earth. The Bible calls it, "its fullness," in Psalm 24:1.

The Man God Made was now ready to resume duty and commence the laying of building blocks, to ensure that Jesus becomes pronounced all over the Earth and beyond. This is why the tower of Babel, in Genesis 11, received a knock-down from God because it was an effort that was jeopardizing the plan of God to turn the entire Earth into where He would come in fellowship with the Man God Made: a place for His recreational presence.

This is the same reason that a new Heaven and Earth will evolve in the end. But the Commander-in-Chief had also already kept in place mansions in Heaven for anyone who would actually complete the task assigned to them here on Earth. The mansions were affluently designed for the spiritual comfort of the Man God Made.

The mansions were really large, and some of the Angels became jealous. The leader of this jealous group was Lucifer (Isaiah 14:12-15), who felt that the only way he could stop man from enjoying the affluence of the mansions was to challenge God over His authority (Ezekiel 28:1), and knowing that our God is a jealous God (Exodus 20:4-5) and an ever-loving God (John 3:16), would rather have him sent down to Earth (Revelation 12:9), where he would now ensure that the Man God Made would continually disobey God (Jeremiah 17:9-10).

He knew that God hates disobedience, and as such God would have nothing to do with the Man God Made but would have him cast out of His sight forever. The devil's only fear was Jesus, the illumination in Heaven and on Earth (Matthew 28:18) and the reason for creation (John 1:1). Would Jesus allow this to happen? The Man God Made was Jesus' own concept of ensuring there was proper order, and the replication of Heavenly values, here on Earth.

The only way the Man God Made could enjoy this affluence would be if Jesus lived with him on Earth and taught him the way of the Commander-in-Chief in Heaven (Matthew 6:9-13). This, to Satan, can never happen, because if Jesus leaves Heaven, the foundation of Heaven will quiver. He was the one holding both the Heavens and the Earth in place. So Satan was very sure that Jesus would not leave Heaven, and as such, the Man God Made would be denied the principles and wisdom of Heaven forever. He was sure that with his reasoning, the Man God Made would never live in affluence, either on Earth or in Heaven. Satan looked at the Earth as the Field Marshall was overcoming the war against every Chaos on Earth (Genesis 1:2). And God was also set to create a special garden for the Man God Made. The plan was displayed everywhere in Heaven. Satan was Jealous as he saw the entire landscape model of the Garden of Eden:

And a river went out of Eden to water the garden; and from thence it was parted, and became into four heads. The name of the first is Pison: that is it which compasseth the whole land of Havilah, where there is gold; And the gold of that land is good: there is bdellium and the onyx stone. And the name of the second river is Gihon: the same is it that compasseth the whole land of Ethiopia. And the name of the third river is Hiddekel: that is it which goeth toward the east of Assyria. And the fourth river is Euphrates. - Genesis 2:10-14

This was too much for the devil to bear. He couldn't hide his jealousy any more. "Will the Man God Made live ever in this affluence while I stay here playing musical instruments and singing? Never!" he argued. There and then, he started the plot to execute the first coup d'état in Heaven. The second act of rebellion was the negligence of duty by the sons of God as they admired the daughters of men and decided to leave Heaven for Earth to takes wives for themselves (Genesis 6:1-5).

Did Adam and Eve ever enjoy this affluence? They only did so for a very short time and then they lost it all to Satan's trick, the same way many of us today are already losing the sonship attribute in us to the tricks of the devil. But if we value affluence, we will not allow the devil to take us out of the path to God's affluence which He has stored in place for the Man God Made.

Let us read Isaiah 45:3:

And I will give thee the treasures of darkness, and hidden riches of secret places, that thou may knowest that I, the Lord, which call thee by name [the Man God Made], am the God of Israel.

This is God's ultimate wish for you and me. Now, looking at this, we could see why King David was called the man after the heart of God. He ensured that he stored enough for the work of God, and for his son Solomon, so that he would not suffer as he ruled over Israel.

We could also see this attribute in the life of Hezekiah the King, who ensured that he cleared out every idolatrous obstacle out of Israel, though when his son Manasseh became king, because he did not value the Lord's affluence, he was led astray (2 Kings 21:1-18). The Bible made us to know that a good man stores riches for his children (Proverbs 13:22):

Do you have this attribute? Are you the one who believes that children should be born for society to train? It is time we had a rethink so that we all can display, in totality, the attributes of the Man God Made.

What therefore are the attributes of a life of affluence?

- It is a life filled with the wisdom and the fear of God (Isaiah 11:1-2).

- It is a life of no denials and all-year-round increase (Genesis 8:22).

- It is a life of unprecedented achievements (Genesis 26:12-16).

- It is a life of exceptional respect and regard for God (Genesis 4:4, Job 1:8, Matthew 5:48).

- It is a life of authority; which is the only way to become fishers of men (Acts 4:1-12).

- It is a life marked with integrity, uprightness and self-discipline (Job 1:8, Job 31:1-40, 1 Corinthians 9:16,24-27).

- It is a life born out of recognition, respect and provision for the needs of spiritual leaders in the church of Christ (1 Corinthians 9:7-14).

CHAPTER THREE

MAN MADE FULL OF LIFE

The Bible says in Genesis 2:7, that God breathed into the man He made and thereafter the Man God Made became a living being (NIV translation). What does this mean? It means He is a man full of life.

The term "being" as represented in "living being" connotes one made for a purpose. The Man God Made is full of vitality, strength and energy. Man was not supposed to be dead unless the Commander-in-Chief withdrew the Field Marshal from protecting and living in him.

And the LORD said, My spirit shall not always strive with man, for that he also is flesh: yet his days shall be an hundred and twenty years - Genesis 6:3.

The man was not supposed to be sick. Jesus confirmed this when He told those He healed that their sins were forgiven them. Now many would argue if all sicknesses are from sin. The answer is yes. For instance, malaria is caused by the bite of the anopheles mosquito, which breeds in a dirty environment, especially stagnant pools of water. Who kept the stagnant waters there? We did, of course! Adam was never sick from malaria, even though rivers compassed the garden, because the rivers were clean and unpolluted. The environment was free of toxins. Polluting the environment is iniquity, because iniquity is the act of wrongdoing.

There is a difference between someone who is existing, simply using their ability to breathe, and someone who is living. Those who live add value to society, while those who exist are no more than additions to the population. Those who only add to the population are those politicians will often deceive with a morsel of bread in order to get their numbers, not vote, because these people don't understand voting rights. They don't yet have a clue what life is all about. These are the ones the devil lies in wait for.

He lies in wait secretly as a lion in his den: he lies in wait to catch the poor: he doth catch the poor, when he draws him into his net. He crouches, and humbles himself, that the poor may fall by his strong ones. He hath said in his heart, God hath forgotten: he hides his face; he will never see it - Psalms 10:9-11.

From what happened later in Genesis 2:19, where Adam named all that God brought to him, we would say that Adam had perfect understanding of what God appreciates (Isaiah 11:3). We are aware that God knows the end from the beginning, which means that He knew the names of each of those animals, but only wanted to confirm the intelligence of the Man God

Made. Naming all the animals created orderliness and an easy means of identification. This is the creative heart combined with intelligent organisation. Are you orderly and organised? Are you the type that meddles things together? If you are not an organised person you are yet to have a perfect understanding of God.

The breath of God we carry is not meant for us just to breathe in oxygen and breathe out carbon dioxide, but to help us to resonate the essence of God's spirit in us. We are a living being, a soul that lives beyond this materialistic world. Our existence on Earth is to use the life we receive from God to add value to our living in such a way that we will not destroy the physical life we have. This is the essence of "being."

From the above discussion we will be explaining what God actually wanted to see in the Man God Made which made Him breathe the breath of life into us. In Genesis 6:3, this breath of God was revealed to be the Spirit of God. We will therefore use this premise to explain what kind of life we ought to be living if we actually have God's Spirit resident in us. Isaiah 11:2 is one verse of the Bible that tries to explain the understanding of the Spirit of God that works in us.

And the spirit of the LORD shall rest upon him, the spirit of wisdom and understanding, the spirit of counsel and might, the spirit of knowledge and of the fear of the LORD; And shall make him of quick understanding in the fear of the LORD: Isaiah 11:2-3.

Verse 3 is highly significant; it says, "Quick

understanding," implying "No Spirit of the Lord, No quick understanding" of God. From here we can enumerate the seven spirits of God to include:

1. The Spirit of The Lord – Leadership.
2. The Spirit of Wisdom – The Light of Life.
3. The Spirit of Understanding - The right application of wisdom.
4. The Spirit of Counsel – Right Judgment.
5. The Spirit of Might – Right focus, dedication, goal driven.
6. The Spirit of Knowledge – Divine information.
7. The Spirit of Fear of the Lord – Respect for authority, obedience and orderliness.

The book of Revelation 1:12 refers to these individual spirits that made up the fullness of the Spirit of God as seven candlesticks. While these lights are in Heaven, we ought to exhibit the attributes of each of these spirits, represented as lights in Heaven, here on Earth. This was the reason behind God commanding Moses to raise seven lamps on a lampstand in the book of Numbers 8:1-4:

And the LORD spoke to Moses, saying: "Speak to Aaron, and say to him, 'When you arrange the lamps, the seven lamps shall give light in front of the lampstand" And Aaron did so; he arranged the lamps to face toward the front of the lampstand, as the LORD commanded Moses. Now this workmanship of the lampstand was hammered gold; from its shaft to its flowers it was hammered work. According to the pattern which the LORD had shown Moses, so he made the lampstand.

The understanding of the facts around the setting up of these lamps will enable us to understand what living a life filled with the Spirit of God is all about.

1. The lamps rest on the lampstand to give light. This is a very important attribute of someone filled with the Spirit of God. The Man God Made is a light to the world. This is why God made Abraham to know that he will be a blessing to others. In Matthew 5:14, Jesus says that the Man God Made is a lamp that cannot be hidden. This is the Spirit of the Lord (Isaiah 11:2). The Man God Made leads by example. The lamps are to give their lights to ensure there is no darkness within the Tabernacle. That is whom we are – showcasing Jesus, the light of God before the world. The Lampstand is therefore symbolic of the vine explained in John 15:1-5. God removes the lampstand (spiritual source of illumination) of whosoever is not bearing abiding fruits from His sight (Revelation 2:4-5): *Nevertheless I have somewhat against thee, because thou hast left thy first love. Remember therefore from whence thou art fallen, and repent, and do the first works; or else I will come unto thee quickly, and will remove thy candlestick (spiritual source of illumination) out of his place, except thou repent – Revelation 2:4-5*

This spiritual source of illumination is likened to a GSM simcard, or what I will refer to as God's Special Messaging Link (GSML), between you and Him. The moment God removes our light-bearing stand from His sight, the devil swings into action to mutilate our lives and in most cases fuses us with a sickness that lasts unto death.

2. The lamps feed from one lampstand which contains the oil. The oil represents the anointing. Each of these lamps cannot exist alone, and cannot be independent of one another. Once any of the lamps go off, we all know what God will do to Aaron and Moses. There will certainly be an attack of plague on the Israelites, because it seems they have not revered God in their midst. The same thing happens when we lack any of these spirits of God. We are denied the fullness of life, and God becomes angry with us, because we will not have "quick understanding" of the things of God. We are all branches of a pure and holy vine - Jesus!

3. The lampstand is made of pure gold. Gold represents divinity. This means that we are supposed to stand out with the divine nature of God in whatsoever we are doing and the world should also see us as representing the divine nature of God. What does this mean? It simply means that we must act like gods (John 10:34).

4. The lampstand is a masterpiece of hammered work. Hammering requires perseverance from the workman, and

this process represents the word of God which we receive from Him in order to become the form that God made (Jeremiah 23:29, John 17:17, John 15:3). It represents the pains we go through to become established as sons of God.

Now, what triggers the seven spirits of God into action is FAITH. When we please God, He comes down to live in us (John 14:15-16,21). Faith, therefore, starts with loving Christ, then obeying His commands, and Christ praying the Father to release the Holy Spirit to live inside of us. And to receive Faith, one has to be taught (Romans 10:17). This process took Jesus three years to teach His disciples. The word of God burns in our hearts to burn away every shaft of sin in us (Luke 24:32). It is only a minister of God burning like a flame of fire that can teach Faith (Hebrews 1:7). The word of God cannot be discerned by any literary judgement (1 Corinthians 2:7).

The sin of Adam and Eve was "faithlessness". This is where Adam lost the faith he had in God, which made him to sin. Before God took that rib from Adam to create Eve, Adam never sinned against God. Adam never complained to God that he needed help; God only saw that it was not good that he should exist alone, with so much potential in him which was lying fallow, since he could not be here and there at the same time. This means that a special part of Adam was missing, and Eve, who represented that better half, was busy being idle with the devil. Amos 3:3 is replayed here to explain why Adam and Eve failed – they never agreed together. If they did, Eve would have had no time to argue about what her husband had told her concerning the tree.

This further points to the fact that Adam may not have recognised the importance of Eve in his life. This is what seldom happens to us. Many of us have prayed and God has answered, but because we are not spiritually intelligent, we still spend long hours fasting and praying. In John 4:10 Jesus opens our understanding to this fact of life. Many of us do not know the gift of life. And I begin to feel that the curse in Jeremiah 17:6 is working against us: ...they will not see prosperity when it comes.

If the Shunemite woman did not have the intelligence to perceive Elisha as a man of God, her son would not come. Even though she was from a well-to-do family, she never looked down on God's servant, as Jehu did when he referred to Elisha as a madman (2 Kings 9:11). If Abraham had not recognised the Angels in Genesis 17, Isaac might not have come as early as that. The Disciples of Jesus met Him to teach them how to pray, because they noticed that there was something unique about the way He was talking with God. The men of the city met Elisha to seek for solution to heal the land, because they knew he had the link to God. To me, Adam was no longer vigilant enough the moment God took that rib from him, and Eve should have complemented his effort.

The serpent coming into the garden without Adam

challenging him as an intruder also shows that the serpent was a regular visitor in that garden, so the devil must have heard all the conversations between God and man. And while God was thinking of getting Adam a helper, the devil must also have heard that, because he too is a spirit. I believe Adam never knew that Eve was meant to complement his effort. I will quickly refer to the book of Genesis 2:22-23: *And the rib, which the LORD God had taken from man, made he a woman, and brought her unto the man. And Adam said, This is now bone of my bones, and flesh of my flesh: she shall be called Woman, because she was taken out of Man.*

From the verses above, we could see that Adam did not wait for God to introduce Eve to him or to tell him why Eve had been made. This is where knowledge comes in. If he had had the knowledge of why Eve was made, he would have also sought to understand what the presence of Eve would do to him, which is in fact the exhibition of the dual functionality of man. Since they are one and the same, they could achieve more, both in the physical and in the spirit.

They were meant to complement one another; instead, Eve was busy talking to an alien who came to admire the beautiful garden they were living in. Today many women are still living as gossipers, dullards, lazy people, lukewarm church members, God-haters, fashion victims, sex workers, etc, because they see themselves as not being part of development or having the opportunity to air their views. This is one of the reasons why today the majority of pastors are now carrying their wives along in the work of ministry. Some women believe it is the responsibility of the husband to put things right all the time, while their own duty is to scatter plans and orders. They quarrel wherever they find themselves. They envy even their fellow womenfolk. They try to please men so that they can be favoured.

Now we should know that the Man God Made is both male and female, and as such the quality of "being" must be displayed by both. A husband and wife are one inseparable entity. The slackness of one means doom for the whole family, then society and finally the world. If many homes can realise that they exist to foster the kingdom of God on Earth, we will reap the beauty of life.

This is why after the fall of man, for us to become the Man God Made, Jeremiah 3:15 says that God will now raise a shepherd who will feed us with knowledge and understanding about the will of God, so that we can build the kind of faith that will please God, and He will come to live in us. The duty of the shepherd is to lead the sheep into a greener pasture where they may graze to maturity, protecting them from the wolf and harsh weather which represent God's verdict of punishment for disobedience and the cunning tricks of the devil. The shepherd must tend the newly born, the sick and weak among them, continuously hoping that one day he will have some without blemish which he can sacrifice to God, and others which would be sold in the market for his upkeep.

The female sheep (ewe) produces more ewes and the shepherd smiles in his heart, because the ewe represents the substance of his increase. We also know that those sheep which wander out of the path of the shepherd's lead become meat for the wolf. What does this explain? The sheep must show total obedience to the instructions of the shepherd to get to the greener pastures, and be safely protected. The female sheep symbolises the evangelists and zealous soul winners. Those sacrificed for God, including their resources, represent members of the congregation who become dedicated to the work of God, some of whom are pastors, deacons, teachers etc.

No one challenges the pastor's decision on whom to dedicate to the work of God, provided God will accept his/her service, which also would represent the sweet savour God smells of every sacrifice. The sheep sold for money represents those who are out there doing business or working for a salary, making returns in cash for the upkeep of the shepherd and his helps and the work of ministry. The resources of the congregation connect them to the covenant between the pastor and God. This is why Abraham has to give a tithe to Melchizedek, the priest of the most High God.

Any shepherd raised by God in line with Jeremiah 3:15 deserves a tithe, which he will spend as ordered by God. How he spends it is his business with God. Abraham didn't bother to ask Melchizedek how he would spend his tithe. Not paying tithes and offerings is stealing from God. And no one eats what belongs to the spirit that will not undergo spiritual affliction. It is like someone eating a sacrifice meant for God, as the sons of Eli did. It is only those who are used by God to communicate events from the spiritual realm to His children who are free to eat spiritual foods.

I have also seen some believers share their tithes among their numerous pastors. You can only have one pastor. Sheep know their shepherd and listen only to his voice. God is not an author of confusion. Tithing shows stewardship towards God and the pastor He has raised for you:

Don't you know that those who serve in the temple get their food from the temple, and that those who serve at the altar share in what is offered on? - 1 Corinthians 9:13 (NIV).

The provision of materials from members to the pastor, and their support to the work of ministry he bears, also connect them to the heart of the pastor. This is what mostly leads to the preservation of such members in the congregation from financial poverty. Most New Testament texts promote giving. 2 Corinthians 9:7 talks about giving cheerfully; 2 Corinthians 8:12 encourages giving what you can afford; 1 Corinthians 16:2 discusses giving weekly, although this is a saved amount for Jerusalem, which could represent giving for annual church events. 1 Timothy 5:18 exhorts supporting the financial needs of Christian workers, Acts 11:29 promotes feeding the hungry wherever they may be, and James 1:27 explains that pure service to God is to help widows and orphans.

Pastors called by God are not hidden. God announces them all around the world, through His signs and wonders, manifesting wherever they go. This is why Jesus says that His disciples are a city set upon a mountain (Matthew 5:13). And the book of Nahum 1:15 says: *Look, there on the mountains, the feet of one who brings good news, who proclaims peace! Celebrate your festivals, Judah, and fulfil your vows. No more will the wicked invade you; they will be completely destroyed. (NIV)*

And, so we can see that we are suppose to celebrate the peace of God when He lives in us. Why can't we have this fullness of life? 1 John 1:5-10 says: *This then is the message which we have heard of him, and declare unto you, that God is light, and in him is no darkness at all. If we say that we have fellowship with him, and walk in darkness, we lie, and do not the truth: But if we walk in the light, as he is in the light, we have fellowship one with another, and the blood of Jesus Christ his Son cleanseth us from all sin. If we say that we have no sin, we deceive ourselves, and the truth is not in us. If we confess our sins, he is faithful and just to forgive us our sins, and to cleanse us from all unrighteousness. If we say that we have not sinned, we make him a liar, and his word is not in us.*

The reason we are unable to live this full life is captured in verse 6: "... do not the truth." The truth is the word of God (John 17:17), yet how many of us follow the truth? How then can we follow the truth when we do not love one another? The only justification for living life to its fullest is our ability to act like God. And to act like God we need His Spirit every day. This implies that we must study, hear and digest the word of God as long as we live. There should be no darkness in our lives. The book of Nahum 1:8 says that God pursues His enemies into the realm of darkness. Are you an enemy of God? No enemy of God should expect peace, except they repent. I have seen that when unbelievers are sorrowful, they go on drinking until they become drunk, in a bid to forget their sorrows, until I saw in the Bible that drunkenness is a punishment from God to the ungodly (Nahum 3:11). So, anyone who gets drunk is under punishment from God because he/she is out of the path of light.

CHAPTER FOUR

MAN MADE BLESSED

God The Commander-in-Chief commanded the Man God Made to take over the leadership of whatsoever belongs to Jesus: the Earth and its fullness and all the powers on Earth and in Heaven.

And God blessed them, and God said unto them, Be fruitful, and multiply, and replenish the Earth, and subdue it: and have dominion over the fish of the sea, and over the fowl of the air, and over every living thing that moveth upon the Earth. - Genesis 1:28

He created them male and female, and He blessed them and named them Man in the day when they were created. - Genesis 5:2 NASB

Every man also to whom God hath given riches and wealth, and hath given him power to eat thereof, and to take his portion, and to rejoice in his labour; this is the gift of God. - Ecclesiastes 5:19

Man was blessed, as a light that should shine forth and facing the world, so as to turn darkness into light. We are made to know that God separated the "light" from the "darkness" in Genesis 1:4, because the light will give shine to the darkness.

This is the duty of man and the whole essence of the blessings upon him. How many of us understand the blessings of God in our lives? We are told that the blessing of God is a fundamental requirement for riches and not sorrows. So we can liken the blessing of the Lord to the wisdom of leadership and divine authority, which forms the foundation for righteous living. And so we could, actually, say that righteousness brings wealth and that unrighteousness brings sorrow.

Now, the blessing of God upon the Man God Made is holistic; which is to say, it is both for the spirit-man and the Earth-man. 3 John 1:2-6 says:

2 Beloved, I wish above all things that thou mayest prosper and be in health, even as thy soul prospereth.

3 For I rejoiced greatly, when the brethren came and testified of the truth that is in thee, even as thou walkest in the truth.

4 I have no greater joy than to hear that my children walk in truth.

5 Beloved, thou doest faithfully whatsoever thou doest to the brethren, and to strangers;

6 Which have borne witness of thy charity before the church: whom if thou bring forward on their journey after a godly sort, thou shalt do well.

We are blessed to bless others and the work of God, hence the Man God Made must prosper both in the physical and in the spirit, as explained in the Bible portion we just read. For a full discussion of the blessings of God upon our lives, you can read chapter five of my book, *The Altar In Golgotha.*

Man lives either a life of blessing or a life of curse (Deuteronomy 30:1). On a daily basis some people are being blessed, and others cursed. Below are the priestly blessings God ordered to be spoken to His covenant children, in Numbers 6:22-27:

22 The LORD said to Moses,

23 "Say to Aaron and his sons, Thus you shall bless the people of Israel: you shall say to them,

24 The LORD bless you and keep you:

25 The LORD make his face to shine upon you, and be gracious to you:

26 The LORD lift up his countenance upon you, and give you peace.

27 "So shall they put my name upon the people of Israel, and I will bless them."

Now let's explain these verses:

- God's servants are given a blessing for you, and they will say it out upon you before God will turn His face towards you to start checking your heart. This is true because wherever a Man of God is, God is there, and so wherever He is standing is automatically the habitation of Angels. When He lifts his voice to call God, the Angels are called to duty immediately. This happens to Elijah (2 Kings 1:10), for instance. As I was writing this, God was showing me how this process happens. It takes less than a second for Him to respond. And we can see this manifested in the life of Daniel, in Daniel 10:12, when the Angel told Daniel:

Then said he unto me, Fear not, Daniel: for from the first day that thou didst set thine heart to understand, and to chasten thyself before thy God, thy words were heard, and I am come for thy words.

The conditions for God intervening in your ill situation are spelt out in this verse: Daniel set his heart to understand, and to keep himself righteous before God. This is what qualified Daniel as a Man of God. And right from the very day he gained an understanding about who God is, his prayers were answered. It is like someone preparing for an examination. Once you are sure that you have completed the academic syllabus for a course, and you understand all that you have studied, there is no way you won't pass your exams. So it is easy to know whether you will be blessed or not, by God.

• The blessings of the Lord must come upon you before He can keep you as His own. And these blessings will make you rich in knowledge, understanding and wisdom. This takes effect after they are said from the mouth of the Man of God, who is in good standing with God (Isaiah 42:1-2). And the favour of the Lord will move into your situation like a cool evening breeze (Genesis 3:8), to give you succour. This is why God will be looking for you as He did Adam. God cannot ignore your tears, because there is 100% joy in Heaven and the will of God must be done on Earth as it is in Heaven. The glory of the Lord fills Heaven with joy. This is why our tears move Him into action. He expects to see joy in our heart as it is in the hearts of the angels in Heaven. As He hears your cry, He also checks your loyalty to Him (Jeremiah 17:10), by checking your heart. Once He finds Satan in your heart, you become defiled (Mark 7:21-22), and He cannot honour the proclamation from the mouth of His servant any more.

On several occasions He had told me the sins of people when they came for counselling, and the reason why they had to repent if they wanted to get His attention. Many people are waiting to hear: it is well with you, without checking through their individual hearts if they have what it takes to receive God.

- Once He keeps you as His own, His face will shine upon you, and then He will be gracious to you. Here He is very confident that your hands are clean. I once had a dream where I saw one of the prophets who have been deceiving people, with his hands covered with stains and looking very dirty. This shows that the fake prophet is doomed already, unless he repents. When we indulge in evil practices, there is no way God's face can shine upon us. His face is Jesus Christ, who is the light of the world. His face shining upon you means that you have been there waiting and looking unto Jesus (Hebrew 12:2), in your situation. You must have repented, returned and waited in the presence of God, fasting and praying. When we are in God's presence, we fear Him and live a sinless life and our joy will spring forth (Exodus 20:20). This is why we need to be in His presence always. Not until the woman bound with infirmity for 18 years sat facing Jesus and hearing Him did she receive her breakthrough (Luke 13:10-13). Once God sees that your heart is filled with remorse for your wrong deeds, and that you know that God is the only source of hope (Hebrew 11:6), you are approved for redemption.

• God will then lift up His countenance, which is His approval of you, before He can give you peace. Here is the basic fact of service. We can see that in the book of Jeremiah 48:10, a curse is upon anyone who will not serve God wholeheartedly: *Cursed be he that doeth the work of the LORD deceitfully.*

How many of us really do the work of God with our hearts? God cannot approve of you when you do not know Him (2 Timothy 2:15). Once you study and pursue His knowledge (Hosea 6:3), He will send His Holy Spirit to dwell in you, so that you do not lead people astray. This is where your pastor comes in (Jeremiah 3:15), to feed you with knowledge and understanding. This is when the Spirit of God will give you "quick understanding" of the meaning of the released oracle.

• And once He approves you as one of His own, who is now heir of His kingdom, you can now be called by His name (2 Chronicles 7:14, Revelations 7:14), and He will finally establish the blessings that were pronounced by His servants upon you. Not until God approves you will these blessings come to pass.

God also told Abraham that he would be a blessing to others, showing that the Man God Made must live with the blessings of God for him to reciprocate them to God's children. This explains why that man can be blessed by God and his fellow humans. But what we see these days is more curses from people, because we are yet to represent God in whatever we do.

Someone could be godly yet not walking with God. This means that the act of godliness does not qualify us as worshipping God in spirit and in truth. Many of us think that our act of welfare alone, without us knowing God and winning souls, will qualify us to reach Heaven. The centurion was godly, yet He was not walking with God in the spirit. Those who walk with God must be zealous for His work (Jeremiah 48:10). We can see this attribute in Phinehas, the son of Aaron, Numbers 25:10-13:

The LORD said to Moses, "Phinehas son of Eleazar, the son of Aaron, the priest, has turned my anger away from the Israelites.

Since he was as zealous for my honour among them as I am, I did not put an end to them in my zeal. Therefore tell him I am making my covenant of peace with him. He and his descendants will have a covenant of a lasting priesthood, because he was zealous for the honour of his God and made atonement for the Israelites." (NIV)

Phinehas had a covenant of peace and that of an everlasting priesthood established in his name by God, because he was zealous for the work of God. Martha was godly, but Mary was both godly and spiritual, and this can be seen in Luke 10:41-42:

"Martha, Martha," the Lord answered, "you are worried and upset about many things, but few things are needed—or indeed only one. Mary has chosen what is better, and it will not be taken away from her." (NIV)

At one time the disciples of Jesus spoke of a godly act; giving to the poor. But Judas, who initiated it, was not spiritual (Matthew 26:7-13). Not until the disciples started carrying out the works of evangelism did they become spiritual as well as godly.

The spiritual side was often the reason why Christ had to explain the scriptures over and over to those He preached to: most of them were Jews who were children of God through the old Mosaic covenant, but they were not spiritual. So the state of godliness does not qualify us to reach Heaven. It is what we confess with our mouths every day that makes our acts of godliness acceptable or not acceptable before God. Those who are godly and spiritual will obey God to the letter in carrying out His instructions of soul winning. To this end, I quickly want to list below four kinds of people:

1. Godly, but not spiritual
2. Godly and spiritual
3. Devilish, but not spiritual
4. Devilish and spiritual

Godly, but not spiritual, people need to be trained on spiritual issues so that they can become spiritual and be empowered with the Holy Spirit to make them both godly and spiritual. The devilish, but not spiritual, sets of people need to be preached to, and they will yield to the gospel. The devilish and spiritual sets of people are more dangerous, as all they do is to fight against the will of God in the church. Spiritual warfare prayers are targeted at this group. They include the witch doctors, witches and wizards, occult members, and their likes.

In the section that follows, we will be treating some of the instances of the blessings from God in the Bible:

GOD BLESSED HIS SABBATH

The Sabbath of the Lord is the day God rested (Genesis 1:22), and as such, God blessed this day, because it is a day for Him to regain His Spirit which had been so busy all the while it took Him to fashion the world the way He wanted. What does this tell us? It puts forward the fact that we all need to bless our source of rest and peace. Jesus says that He is the Lord of the Sabbath, meaning that He was actually the one God blessed on that Sabbath, and anyone who is cleaved to Him will definitely receive the Lord's blessings.

GOD BLESSED MAN

By the act of approval and contentment from God, He blessed everything that He created, until finally at the end of creation He created the Man God Made in His own image, to live a very short life span – from his creation to when God caused a deep sleep to fall upon him. Then He blessed them (Genesis 1:28), desiring for them the best out of the world He had made.

GOD BLESSED ALL THAT HE MADE

I decided to talk about the Sabbath of the Lord first, because it is the only day that God proclaimed as Holy unto Him. Why would God bless all that He had created? Simply put: to make them perfect. The blessings of the Lord bring riches with no regrets (Proverbs 10:22). It was a time for progress review, a time of contemplation and a day filled with the spirit of triumph. It was joy that the world which was once chaotic could receive light to experience perfection through Jesus Christ. It was the joy in the Heart of God that blessed all that He created - at the end of each day, when He had finished a specific element of His creation. And finally, God saw everything that He had made, and it was glowing in perfection. The King James version of the Bible rendered the original Hebrew word, "towb," as "very good," meaning from Strong's Number H2896, "perfect in order or beautiful." This very act of God in Genesis 1:31 corrected any form of imperfection that would have existed after creation. You are perfect, I am perfect, and everything around us is perfect. This is God's intention and design.

In our next discussion we will look at how a curse came into the life of man.

THE CURSE UPON MAN

We will also see the curse laid on The Man God Made, and what led to his falling into sin. I am only re-emphasizing this so that it will take root within our consciousness.

The Man God Made was created to know only the goodness and the love of God, so that they could bless Him and show gratitude to Him alone, daily, for the wealth of His blessings all over the Earth. The Man God Made was immortal in nature, in body and soul by God's divine decree, being created according to the holy nature of God in purity and holiness.

Until that day when Adam and Eve sinned by eating the fruit of the tree of the knowledge of good and evil, God's will for them was for the Man God Made not to taste death.

God's anger against them and the serpent shows how disappointed He was. There and then God started the rescue mission that would save the Man God Made from eternal destruction by first sacrificing an animal to clothe his nakedness. And this act also points to the fact that when we put on the person of Christ as our garment, we will certainly be covered from shame.

Obedience is a price we usually pay up front, unlike sin, which is like buying on credit or taking a loan. The effects of sin burns us into ashes when we least expect it by making our hearts experience guilt.

Sin was disguised as bait in the beauty of that apple in the garden, and the Man God Made fell for it, losing his spiritual relationship with God.

To me this was the curse upon the Man God Made. The punishment for disobedience is often the opposite of the beauty of attraction; meaning that once we disobey God's instructions we will no longer be focused in life.

It may be hard to believe, but when people commit sins they wear a foul-smelling garment in the spirit, and people usually start avoiding them.

Sin infuriates God, and so it does anyone who has the spirit of God at heart.

THE WORLD AT SIN

The "very good" approval from God in Genesis 1:31 received a reversal knock of discontentment from God after that man had sinned. And man became like an engine that is seized up with all its moving parts after experiencing wear and tear. Many of the blessings that God had bestowed upon creation were revoked, just as a medical doctor's licence would be withdrawn for lack of competence. The Man God Made was treated with disparagement and flippancy for his sins by the host of Heaven. He was treated like a pig in mud. He would have to toil in sweat in order to survive. To make matters worse, the Earth would grow thorns and thistles. The world became an unfriendly place for the Man God Made to dwell in. This was the manifestation of the proclamation of woe upon the Earth, in Revelation 12:12.

GOD IS WILLING TO RESTORE MANKIND

After this era, as we discussed earlier, God in His infinite mercy provided an opportunity for anyone who would want to become the Man God Made, to repent, in order that he might obtain His blessings through Jesus Christ. Hence Christ cried out in John 7:37: *On the last day, that great day of the feast, Jesus stood and cried out, saying, "If anyone thirsts, let him come to Me and drink. He who believes in Me, as the Scripture has said, out of his heart will flow rivers of living water."* But this He spoke concerning the Spirit, whom those believing in Him would receive;... and the process of receiving the Holy Spirit has to do with Christ revealing to us all the purpose of God in our lives as espoused by Jesus in Matthew 11:27-29: *All things have been delivered to Me by My Father, and no one knows the Son except the Father. Nor does anyone know the Father except the Son, and the one to whom the Son wills to reveal Him. Come to Me, all you who labour and are heavy laden, and I will give you rest. Take My yoke upon you and learn from Me, for I am gentle and lowly in heart, and you will find rest for your souls. For My yoke is easy and My burden is light.*

For this to take effect in our lives, the book of Revelation 1:3 says: *Blessed is he who reads and those who hear the words of this prophecy, and keep those things which are written in it; for the time is near.*

This portion we read tells us that whoever reads or hears and keep the word of God is blessed. Jesus also says in John 20:29: *...Blessed are those who have not seen and yet have believed.*

Do you want to be blessed? You should know what to do by now, from the Bible verses referred to above. The Man God Made is therefore:

1. One who seeks the knowledge of God through the study of the Bible and hearing the teachings from God's servants.
2. One who believes them, without looking for a proof through signs and miracles.
3. One who keeps the word, as one is not supposed to be only a hearer, but a doer of God's command.

The pain we go through today was never intended by God. The consequences of the sin we commit daily continue to be a thorn in our flesh that must be taken away. We must come to the Lord Jesus to experience God's forgiveness and to partake in the blessings that were originally meant for the Man God Made.

In dishonour, tears and pain we were born – our mothers were naked with their legs wide open for the doctor(s) and nurse(s) to see the nakedness they had treasured so much, and all manner of medical instruments would be inserted into her, in some cases. Worse still, with dishonour, tears and pain we depart this world – many would foam in their mouth on their dying bed. And as a punishment for the sin of man, our daily bread must be asked for, from God - it was never so in the beginning. Man had everything available for him in the garden. In most cases, our Earthly suffering today is connected with our search for daily bread – what a shame.

The Mercy of God in Christ sends a message of repentance into our hearts (Galatians 4:6) once we realise that we are going the way of extermination. This promise is contained in the Lord's deliverance "white paper" which opened with the declaration:

For God so loved the world, that he gave his only begotten Son, that whosoever believeth in him should not perish, but have everlasting life. - John 3:16

The use of the word, "For" at the beginning of that verse refers to the expectation of God when we repent, that we will all become the Man God Made: a man filled with everlasting life, A life that transcends above this physical plain.

This is the assurance of an everlasting freedom, a path of an everlasting walk with God which will make us the creator's creation: the Man God Made.

The following instances buttresses the fact that God is still ever ready to ensure that we are blessed in Him.

Enoch's Blessing

Enoch lived three hundred and sixty-five years. He was among those blessed by God, because he walked with God. The Bible recorded in Genesis 5:24 that he never experienced physical death. Methuselah, one of his sons, is acclaimed as the man with the longest life on Earth: nine hundred and sixty-nine years. Methuselah's grandson through Lamech, Noah, was born with a promise of deliverance, as the name suggests:

And he called his name Noah, saying, This same shall comfort us concerning our work and toil of our hands, because of the ground which the Lord hath cursed. Genesis 5:29

Noah's Blessing

Noah found favour in the sight of God, because he was a righteous man who walked with God, at a time when humanity was already living in the well of sin as a result of their increasing number, as is being experienced today in the world. The Bible says:

And it came to pass, when men began to multiply on the face of the Earth, and daughters were born unto them, That the sons of God saw the daughters of men that they were fair; and they took them wives of all which they chose. And the Lord said, My spirit shall not always strive with man, for that he also is flesh: yet his days shall be an hundred and twenty years. There were giants in the Earth in those days; and also after that, when the sons of God came in unto the daughters of men, and they bare children to them, the same became mighty men which were of old, men of renown. And God saw that the wickedness of man was great in the Earth, and that every imagination of the thoughts of his heart was only evil continually. And it repented the Lord that he had made man on the Earth, and it grieved him at his heart. And the Lord said, I will destroy man whom I have created from the face of the Earth; both man, and beast, and the creeping thing, and the fowls of the air; for it repenteth me that I have made them. But Noah found grace in the eyes of the Lord. Genesis 6:1-8

Thereafter, God instructed him to raise a new generation of humans and animals for Him. The Bible told us that Noah was mocked, because what he was saying could only be seen as the ranting of a madman – well so it seemed in their ears, since nothing like this had happened in history. Then he swung into action, raising a tabernacle in the form of a ship unto God, as he was commanded by God: *Thus Noah did; according to all that God commanded him, so he did (Genesis 6:22).*

The rains did come upon the Earth, and he and his family made it into the new world, as voyagers of a new order. He made a sacrifice that pleased God and he was blessed – thus, making Noah the father of modern-day man. Today we are still enjoying the elements of that blessing: Be fruitful and multiply, and fill the Earth (Genesis 9:1).

Though Noah injected curse into the world when he cursed his grandson – Canaan (Genesis 9:18-24), God has never stopped to bless those who walk with Him in uprightness, since then.

Our next discussion is a summary of what I feel is responsible for man's inability to attain the status of the Man God Made, who lives with the blessings of God.

1. Lack of love – this is characterised by envy, jealousy, hatred, backbiting, covetousness and the likes. Love is about care. It is about provision for the needy in our midst:

Genesis 9:18: but you shall remember that you were a slave in Egypt and the Lord your God redeemed you from there; therefore I command you to do this.

19: When you reap your harvest in your field, and have forgotten a sheaf in the field, you shall not go back to get it; it shall be for the sojourner, the fatherless, and the widow; that the Lord your God may bless you in all the work of your hands.

20: When you beat your olive trees, you shall not go over the boughs again; it shall be for the sojourner, the fatherless, and the widow.

21: When you gather the grapes of your vineyard, you shall not glean it afterward; it shall be for the sojourner, the fatherless, and the widow.

*22: You shall remember that you were a slave in the land of Egypt;
therefore I command you to do this.*

Before we became born again, we were sinners, and now that
we have Christ in our lives, if we truly love sinners the way
Christ did, we would become effective soul winners, through
the show of charity within our neighbourhood. If out of the
eater came something to eat (Judges 14:14), we that are the
proponents of salvation should do more than give something
for others to eat, provide more than just food. The Bible says
that the poor had the gospel preached to them (Matthew
11:5). We can't deny them the gospel of Christ. And while
we do this in our missionary works, we should include welfare
items that will bring them physical comfort.

2. Disobedience to the instruction of God is a deadly sin. This
is what breeds murmuring. We murmur because of lack of
understanding. The preacher says in Ecclesiastes 5:2:

*Be not rash with thy mouth, and let not thine heart be hasty to
utter anything before God: for God is in Heaven, and thou upon
Earth: therefore let thy words be few.*

Anyone who murmurs does not regard God, and as such God
will certainly visit such a person with His anger. No one can
withstand the fury of God. Not even Moses could withstand
it. Our sins are what makes us run for cover any time we see
lightning in the sky or hear thunder strike.

3. Our failure to bless God is seen by God as ingratitude to Him. When we fail to bless God before the congregation and unbelievers, how can we claim to exist as God's image and likeness? Let us learn from the man after the heart of God, in the following Psalms:

135:19 Bless the Lord, O house of Israel: bless the Lord, O house of Aaron.

135:20 Bless the Lord, O house of Levi: you that fear the Lord, bless the Lord.

135:21 Blessed be the Lord out of Zion, who dwell in Jerusalem

145:1 I will extol you, O God my king: and I will bless your name for ever; yea, forever and ever.

145:2 Every day I will bless you: and I will praise your name for ever; yea, for ever and ever.

145:10 Let all your works, O Lord, praise you: and let your saints bless you.

145:21 My mouth shall speak the praise of the Lord: and let all flesh bless your holy name for ever; yea, for ever and ever.

With all these, we could see why God was so proud of David. Every one of us should learn to praise, adore, honour and bless the Lord. Why do we need to bless Him?

For he commanded, and they [we] were created, and because He has strengthened the bolts of your gates, He has blessed your children within you. - Psalms 148:5,13.

4. Idolatry has eaten deep into the hearts of this generation. Obscene images are displayed everywhere the head turns. We have decided to travel round the world and visit evil cultures, which we now accept as right before God. Instead of correcting wrongs, we now preach their acceptance. Whoredom is eating deep into our souls – there are brothels all over the place. Marriages are being torn apart and children are left to roam the streets as orphans; yet many of us have decided to sit in churches with air-conditioning units blowing on us, without taking out a day to preach the gospel of repentance to this generation. Many pastors are smiling to the banks, and would rather spend offerings in travelling abroad and living in expensive hotels instead of buying out all the business empires and forcing the world to accept the only available means of survival if we do the former: which is working in a Christian organisation, because that would be all that existed. I am not comfortable that believers will go seeking a job in a firm established by idolatry practitioners. I am also not comfortable with believers sitting before ungodly men to be appraised in an interview setting.

The choice is ours to make today. Deuteronomy 30:16-20 says:

16 If you obey the commandments of the Lord your God which I command you this day, by loving the Lord your God, by walking in his ways, and by keeping his commandments and his statutes and his ordinances, then you shall live and multiply, and the Lord your God will bless you in the land which you are entering to take possession of it.

17 But if your heart turns away, and you will not hear, but are drawn away to worship other gods and serve them,

18 I declare to you this day, that you shall perish; you shall not live long in the land which you are going over the Jordan to enter and possess.

19 I call Heaven and Earth to witness against you this day, that I have set before you life and death, blessing and curse; therefore choose life, that you and your descendants may live,

20 Loving the Lord your God, obeying his voice, and cleaving to him; for that means life to you and length of days, that you may dwell in the land which the Lord swore to your fathers, to Abraham, to Isaac, and to Jacob, to give them.

CHAPTER FIVE

MAN MADE A GOVERNOR

The Man God Made was kept in God's own garden in order to tend it and give it the kind of facelift that would impress God. The daily overseeing of the garden was his own responsibility, and the Commander-in-Chief only came into the garden to obtain status reports from him, and to see if the man was having any challenges that would hinder his performance. This points to the fact that the Man God Made was made by God to:

- Live for God: *Let us hear the conclusion of the whole matter: Fear God, and keep his commandments: for this is the whole duty of man - Ecclesiastes 12:13.*

- Live in God: *For I know the thoughts that I think toward you, saith the LORD, thoughts of peace, and not of evil, to give you an expected end - Jeremiah 29:11.*

- Live with God: *I am the true vine, and my Father is the husbandman. Every branch in me that beareth not fruit he taketh away: and every branch that beareth fruit, he purgeth it, that it may bring forth more fruit - John 15:1-2.*

- Live by God: *The steps of a good man are ordered by the LORD: and he delighteth in his way. Though he fall, he shall not be utterly cast down: for the LORD upholdeth him with his hand* - Psalm 37:24-24.

- Live as God: *For if ye love them which love you, what reward have ye? do not even the publicans the same? And if ye salute your brethren only, what do ye more than others? do not even the publicans so? Be ye therefore perfect, even as your Father which is in Heaven is perfect* - Matthew 5:46-48.

He is a Man of God, and not the likeness of the man who was hiding from King Achish (1 Samuel 21:13-15, Psalm 37:1-2). A Man of God is called by the name of God (2 Chronicles 7:14, Psalm 89:18-20), who is bold enough to stand as a Holy vessel unto God all the time, no matter what challenges of life they may face. David was afraid in the verses above because he was yet to understand who lived inside him. Even as a mighty man of war, David was occasionally afraid of his enemies, and he even fled from Saul (1 Samuel 20:1-10) and his own son, Absalom, for the purpose of seeking safety (Psalm 3:1). Elijah had to flee from Jezebel, in 1 Kings 19. Are these the likeness of the Man God Made? Once Peter was empowered with the Holy Spirit, he became bolder than ever (Acts 2). The Lord has not given us the spirit of fear. Rather He has given us the spirit of governorship.

The term "Man of God" does not represent some sets of

individuals only, but it is always the intention of God that all men shall be called by His name, because they were to be inspired by Him alone. It became a popular term, because sin had taken over the entirety of man, and God now searches for anyone He could call His own, who will be ready to take up the job of restoration (Isaiah 42:22). The term "man", as used in this book, does not refer to the male only, but rather to both male and female in line with God's declaration in Genesis 1:26-27. We can see that in verse 26, God referred to the term "man" in the plural form when He said, "let them." It is the tradition that sons are heirs to their parents and so in God's Kingdom there is neither male nor female, husband nor wife – we are all sons of the kingdom (Galatians 3:28). Sonship is an attribute of partnership with God. This is the status of the Man God Made.

There are qualities and rules that the Man God Made must adhere to for effective governance to become possible. Will he fulfil these? Will he ever rule as God intended from the beginning? Jesus lived a life that convinced everyone that He was, indeed, from Heaven, and they wanted to make Him king by force (John 6:15), after He had fed a multitude who were about Him.

So, if man is made to be a governor, why are there grumblings in society over the acts of leadership worldwide? The answer is - unrighteousness. Man decided to build on a wrong foundation and as such we can no longer lead as God expected of us. Happiness and peace will visit the Earth when the righteous is in power (Proverbs 29:2), but the Bible says no one is righteous yet (Psalms 14:1-3).

Man was supposed to be a cadet Commander-in-Chief who should have taken full control of the world God handed over to him. The Bible says that just as through one man sin entered into the world, so also through one man sin departed from the world (Roman 5:12). This means that any time we are forgiven of our sins we may lead effectively (John 1:29).

There are three responsibilities that the world sees as the duty of a governor: ceremonial, legislative and general duties. I have added a fourth; spiritual duty. The Man God Made is responsible for ensuring that these duties are adequately carried out, without lapses – whether at home, in the office or in the church. These duties are explained below:

Ceremonial Duties

The performance of ceremonial duties is an avenue to foster unity, love, and dedication to the service of belief and faith among the people. Priests wear special headgear to enable them to perform their ceremonial duties (Exodus 28:39). When we minister to people, praying, counselling them, sanctuary keeping, welfare, and whatsoever will minister good into the lives of people, we are carrying out our ceremonial duties.

And the LORD God took the man, and put him into the garden of Eden to dress it and to keep it. Gen. 2:15

In the church for instance, the pastor can assign various duties to other people with the capacity to do that as seen in the book of Acts 6:2-3: *Then the twelve called the multitude of the disciples unto them and said, It is not reason that we should leave the word of God, and serve tables. Wherefore, brethren, look ye out among you seven men of honest report, full of the Holy Ghost and wisdom, whom we may appoint over this business.*

Such persons must be approved by God as also seen in Exodus 35:30-35: *And Moses said unto the children of Israel, See, the LORD hath called by name Bezaleel the son of Uri, the son of Hur, of the tribe of Judah; And he hath filled him with the spirit of God, in wisdom, in understanding, and in knowledge, and in all manner of workmanship; And to devise curious works, to work in gold, and in silver, and in brass, And in the cutting of stones, to set them, and in carving of wood, to make any manner of cunning work. And he hath put in his heart that he may teach, both he, and Aholiab, the son of Ahisamach, of the tribe of Dan. Them hath he filled with wisdom of heart, to work all manner of work, of the engraver, and of the cunning workman, and of the embroiderer, in blue, and in purple, in scarlet, and in fine linen, and of the weaver, even of them that do any work, and of those that devise cunning work.*

No man can work in God's vineyard except approved

through deep study of His ways (2 Timothy 2:15). To tend means to put in order, in the form that it would be originally, or perform in accordance with the original intention of the creator, or owner. To tend is to preserve. This is the essence of our ceremonial duties as children of the new covenant in Christ.

Legislative Duties
Legislation has to do with the making of law. Moses' first point of order was his meeting with God to hear the Ten Commandments and help him lead. King Solomon also, went to God for wisdom to help him rule. This involves abiding by the constitution of the church of Christ which our Lord commands in the Bible, to win souls for the kingdom of God (John 20:21). In the church, the rules and regulations which have been put in place to ensure that there is order in service, and the codes of conducts of particular departments in the church aimed at maintaining order in our worship to God, are all legislative duties. In our families we also make rules and regulations to ensure that our children and our household are led right to serve God.

And out of the ground the LORD God formed every beast of the field, and every fowl of the air; and brought them unto Adam to see what he would call them: and whatsoever Adam called every living creature, that was the name thereof. Gen 2:19

Legislative duties help us to decree things and see them

come to pass. This is the intention of God towards man. Without us performing our God-assigned legislative duties, there is no way we can put things in order. When we give our children names, we want to see them living those names. The names we give to our businesses will show how far they will strive. Many companies worldwide don't survive long because they are registered with terminating names. This is where wisdom comes to play – to effectively perform this duty, we must have a perfect knowledge of God and His creations around us.

As a king, Solomon studied the ways of the ants (Proverbs 6:6), in order to help him put a pattern of work in place for those working with him. In the Book of Psalms we can also see that David's psalms are a reflection of his understanding of the universe, and how he relates their existence to the presence of God. This may also be the reason why he succeeded in his legislative duty as a king.

General Duties

Striving to live your destiny and fulfilling your purpose on Earth, daily, is your general duty. God sent us to overcome the world. This means that we must strive to succeed in life wherever we are, and in whatever we do.

And God blessed them, and God said unto them, Be fruitful, and multiply, and replenish the Earth, and subdue it: and have dominion over the fish of the sea, and over the fowl of the air, and over every living thing that moveth upon the Earth. Genesis 1:28

If we carry out this duty as believers, the world will not slip out of our hands into the mud of sin. Unbelievers will run to us to lead them to our source of success. The problem we are having is that we hardly seek the right wisdom to enable us do the will of God, so that our day-to-day living will experience the peace of God. The wisdom of God is all we need to achieve the purpose of this duty. The Bible says in Jeremiah 8:9: *The wise men are ashamed, they are dismayed and taken: lo, they have rejected the word of the LORD; and what wisdom is in them.*

If we don't want shame to come upon us, all we need to do to carry out this duty is to seek after the wisdom of God.

Spiritual Duties
This duty helps us to connect to God at all times. This includes studying the Word, praying, fasting, worship, praise, and adoration of God. It is the desire of God that we connect with Him every time so that His spirit can dwell in our hearts, and causing us to exercise the gift of salvation more and more. We can get the elements of this duty in the following Bible passages: *And the LORD God commanded the man, saying, of every tree of the garden thou mayest freely eat: But of the tree of the knowledge of good and evil, thou shalt not eat of it: for in the day*

that thou eatest thereof thou shalt surely die. - Genesis 2:16-17

Let us hear the conclusion of the whole matter: Fear God, and keep his commandments: for this is the whole duty of man. For God shall bring every work into judgment, with every secret thing, whether it be good, or whether it be evil. - Ecclesiastes 12:13-14

In Isaiah 42:16 God says He will lead us. What we should be thinking now is whether we have submitted to His leading. If we fail to allow God to lead us, then we will not make Heaven and we will also live a life of complaints.

The Man God Made failed in the last duty and all the other duties began collapsing. This is what happens when we fail in our spiritual responsibilities, which is supposed to make us righteous. When the righteous rule, the people will surely rejoice. This is the truth! How are we taking our spiritual responsibilities seriously? Do we need someone to chase us around, or do we pay lip service to God's instructions? The Bible says God brought every living creature to Adam, and he named them. Was he only satisfying God when God was around, or did he have the fear of God? Adam's fall confirms that he did the latter. If you are a mother, do the children behave well only when your husband is around? Have we gone the way of most Nigerian state governors, who take the president only to the places where social amenities seems to be partially in order, while there is chaos all over the rest of the state?

If we actually take a look at the duties explained above, we will be able to know that right from the home front a lot of work is still to be done. If the home lives according to the will of God, then the church will live according to the will of God, and then society will be a better place for all of us. As we have seen, the Man God Made is supposed to be a responsible man, with the emblem of honour and glory manifesting wherever they go. This is where seeking knowledge is very important.

Whether you are a male or female, it is time to outline our responsibilities and duties on a daily basis. The husband should prayerfully know where God wants him to be, and the wife should prayerfully confirm that God's hand is really in what they are about to do, then both of them must also prayerfully, accordingly to their talents, draw out their responsibilities, to ensure that they succeed together as one flesh.

Why are we not able to drive through the process of leadership? Many factors are responsible, among which could be the lack of the fear of God, lack of trust in God, lack of adequate knowledge and understanding, too much drive for worldliness (Luke 12:34), etc. See what Moses father-in-law told him:

And thou shalt teach them ordinances and laws, and shalt show them the way wherein they must walk, and the work that they must do. Moreover thou shalt provide out of all the people able men, such as fear God, men of truth, hating covetousness; and place such over them, to be rulers of thousands, and rulers of hundreds, rulers of fifties, and rulers of tens: And let them judge the people at all seasons: and it shall be, that every great matter they shall bring unto thee, but every small matter they shall judge: so shall it be easier for thyself, and they shall bear the burden with thee - Exodus 18:20-22.

The question we should be asking ourselves now is if we have the spiritual qualities explained in verse 21: *Moreover thou shalt provide out of all the people able men, such as fear God, men of truth, hating covetousness...*

In the latter part of that verse you will see that this governorship responsibility is from the family first. How do we solve problems? Do we really have what it takes to handle issues in the home before coming to the church? Many of us are good at crying to God to solve problems for us when we could have solved it within the home easily.

What I see lacking is the attribute of governorship which we lost as a result of Adam's sin. But now that we are in Christ, we should begin to think of how we can fulfil our duties as governors of whatsoever garden God has entrusted to our care.

In summary, we can say that the failure of man to carry out the duties of a governorship placed on him by God is due to the following:

CHAPTER FIVE

1. Lack of Ownership

Why should Adam allow an alien to control his household for him? Why should he have allowed the serpent into the garden when it was supposed to be in the field? The garden was not the serpent's home. Many men today are unable to take ownership of their home. The children are allowed to watch any kind of movie. Their wives may have any kind of friends. Family secrets fly all around, and the supposed man of the house stands with arms akimbo, watching the devil take over the ownership of his home.

Again, Adam failed to be the Man God Made when he couldn't take responsibility for what happened in that garden. Instead he was blaming his wife, who was new to the garden and not used to all the strange visitors that strolled into the garden without him cautioning them. Women always borrow a leaf from the man they are married to, and if the man fails, there is every certainty that the woman may fail, unless she has a prior knowledge of God in her.

If we take a look at Abraham, who lied to save his life, we would notice that Sarah took decisions that would not be expected from someone who is godly: she forced Haggai into Abraham's life, and then made Abraham push her maid out of the house without a care for what would happen to Ishmael. Again, we see Rebecca hating her own son, Esau. This would also be measured side by side with Isaac's decision to bless Esau against his marriage to a Canaanite woman.

Jacob's two wives turned Jacob into a "sexaholic" who had to sleep with their maid in order to fulfil their desires and ended up turning Jacob's home into a home of hatred.

When I look into what happened to Lot's wife, who disobeyed God, I would also place her act side by side with Lot's act of dishonour against Abraham when they had a dispute. The Bible told us that the presence of Joseph in Potiphar's house brought them the blessings of God, but his wife threw all that out with her desire to sleep with Joseph (Genesis 39:1-20). The Bible says in Proverbs 14:1 that a woman is instrumental to what happens to her home: good or bad. A woman wanting to please her husband often changes her godly attributes to her husband's worldly agenda in order to keep her home. I have seen women who drink themselves into a stupor because their husbands do so.

A man should protect his home, and the woman should know that without the right wisdom, there is no way her home can be put together. Instead of them going about trying to make themselves look more sexy, which only lasts as long as the man appreciates it, they should yield more to knowing about God.

Every woman must take ownership today. The heart of a woman is deeper than the deepest sea. She can keep secrets for ages, and usually die with them. This is one of the reasons for women's inability to yield fully to God. Sometime they also live a life of suspicion. They value their husbands in most cases above God, and when they are not getting the attention of their husbands as they expected, and especially if what they want contravenes godly principles, they would turn to fake prophets and witch doctors. Many can keep their children's misdeeds from their husband's knowledge, but will not hesitate to expose their husband's weak points to the public and thereby expose their homes to the spiritual cobwebs that now mask every member of the family.

2. Lack of Defence

Adam should have defended His home against the devil's attack. This is where many of us lose our homes and authority to our enemies. As long as God has anointed us with authority, we should be aware that the enemy will use those who are close to us to attack our vision, if they cannot get at us.

What we must do is equip those who bear our vision with us with the right knowledge and wisdom, and encourage them to seek understanding of the knowledge that is in their hearts whenever they are in doubt. They should know the rules and regulations of the setting before them by heart. They should be taught continually. This is the whole essence of indoctrination and on-the-job training.

Our families and those that work with us must know about the recent technological innovations in the world, while we explain to them the advantages and the disadvantages of applying them in our lives. For instance, our children should be exposed to sex education in good time and taught the spiritual implications of premarital sex. We should go the extra mile to explain all aspects of sex; from oral sex to homosexual acts, fondling, breast sucking, touching by the opposite sex, "smooching", etc. Children should be taught godly business principles in time, and especially how to save money and making wise investments, before they sell their souls to the devil. They should know the implication of the sin of cheating, lying, backbiting, etc. Knowing the root of all the woes in the Bible is a very good starting point. Filter out all the woes and curses in the Bible using Bible software search engines, and take time out, as the adult in the home, to study them, and later to explain them to your family and those who work under you. That way, once they all have the fear of God in their hearts, you will not experience failure.

3. Inability to Harness the Natural Resources of the Garden

I have found that it is always the stranger who discovers the hidden treasures in our lives first, before we realise we have such gifts in us. This is why many of us have become stooges in the hands of labour employers. Many of us have talents that we have not tapped.

Let us take a look at the fruit of the forbidden tree in that garden. Not until Satan had made Eve take a second look at the fruits of that tree did she see the beauty in that fruit. And because of her new desire, she couldn't resist the temptation of having to taste it.

Every woman should know that she is beautiful and not that she should be waiting for a man or for someone else to tell her how beautiful she is. I met a woman one day and told her she was beautiful. She acknowledged it and left. Later that day she called me to invite me to lunch because of that compliment, and she confessed that her husband always said she was ugly. For days, she was calling me to have lunch so that I could continue to tell her she was beautiful. She changed her hairstyle frequently to ensure she earned the compliment on a daily basis. If I had not been self-disciplined that could have started us on a date, and then we would have committed adultery.

Discover who you are. Don't wait for others to tell you that you are beautiful before you know that you are. Don't dress to impress others. Many young women have asked me how they should dress, and my answer would be to imitate Mary, the mother of Jesus. She is the only woman who found favour with God, and prophesied that all generations shall call her blessed. Jesus grew in her womb for nine months, showing that she is an emblem of purity and perfection. Her holy and righteous life should be emulated by all women. Any woman who would not emulate the qualities of Mary, the mother of Jesus, can never be claiming to know God. Such a woman is, rather, a daughter of Eve.

Mary was never seen talking with any other man or creature as Eve did, because that would have been Joseph's first point of suspicion; she only spoke with God's Angel. How did Mary dress? She wasn't putting on a man's apparel, I'm sure, because she would have been stoned to death by the Jewish authorities. Let your appearance bless God, and become part of your Christian life, rather than dressing to impress others. You are fearfully and wonderfully made. You are the image of God. Accept yourself, rather than waiting for others to do so. Don't live your life on what people admire. Live your life to please God.

Another thing I also saw in that Garden of Eden was that despite the enormous wealth of minerals present there, there was no reference that Adam tried to figure out what to do with them. It took the grandchildren of Cain to start invention (Genesis 4: 21-22). We need to discover ourselves early, and to have a deep knowledge about what is present in our socio-spiritual environment, instead of waiting for someone else with the devil's intention to do it for us. We are told:

Whatsoever thy hand findeth to do, do it with thy might; for there is no work, nor device, nor knowledge, nor wisdom, in the grave, whither thou goest. Ecclesiastes 9:10

4. Lack of Family Fellowship

If the family fellowship ever existed, the spiritual consciousness of Eve would have been alert, because she would be thinking of her husband's reaction when he discovered what she was doing with the serpent. I believe that since this was weak, neither of them could really show that they feared God. If they had done, Adam would have resisted his wife. Today our family altars are empty because we don't share fellowship together all the time. There is an absence of the word of God in our homes. Many of us only confess Jesus in church, not in public or in our homes.

We can talk football, but not Christ. Souls are perishing daily and we are keeping quiet. In the revelation God showed me on the 3rd of December 2011, in the judgement that was going on in that court of God, no one could make Heaven. This is a call to each and every one of us to preach the word. We are told that faith is implanted in our hearts through continuous hearing (Romans 10:17). This, I guess, was lacking in Adam's home, so Eve had no faith in God. This is the reason for her easily succumbing to the plots of the devil.

5. Failure In Reproductive Responsibility

Adam only knew his wife after they left the garden: *And Adam knew Eve his wife; and she conceived. - Genesis 4:1.*

What were they doing that did not allow them time for

intercourse? This points to the fact we discussed earlier. He didn't take time to get closer to his wife, to her thoughts and desires. There is a portion of the Bible that is very helpful in marriage, and this is Ecclesiastes 9:9:

Live joyfully with the wife whom thou lovest all the days of the life of thy vanity, which he hath given thee under the sun, all the days of thy vanity: for that is thy portion in this life, and in thy labour which thou takest under the sun.

The Bible also says, in Ecclesiastes 4:11, that when two sleep together they keep themselves warm. When a man and a woman sleep together, the warmth that results must lead to discovery and then to copulation. What happened in their own case? They may have even been sleeping separately, or Adam may have been busy counting the stars at night, or maybe, because he didn't wait for God to introduce the woman properly before he exclaimed in that fantasy, he may not have been aware of the purpose of Eve in his life. We said earlier that we need to discover everything around us on time – we must know the inherent potentials in our wives, children, friends, neighbours and so on. This way, we will become productive in life.

We have so much authority in our hands, but before we can harness them for our good we need to seek the wisdom of God. The discussion we will be having in the next chapter is how we can develop our strength to help us become the Man God Made.

CHAPTER SIX

MAN MADE FULL OF STRENGTH

To me, when the going gets tough, the tough should simply ignore the going and settle with Jesus. The Lord once told me that those who make things happen don't struggle. Before Adam's sin, there was no struggle in his life; God ensured that he was healthy and happy with all the wealth in the Garden of Eden. In John 14:18, Jesus says that He will not abandon us to the extent that we become orphans. He is right here with you, standing there as you read this piece. May the good Lord grant you peace this moment. Amen.

Until man sinned against God he did not need to look for God, because God lives inside him. Christ let us know that he would not leave us as orphans. After His resurrection, he appeared to His disciples three times. We are unable to exercise the power of God in us because we are in sin. If you see yourself looking for God, you need to wake up.

The disciples waited in the upper room and were endowed with strength from above. They sacrificed all the hours it took them to wait for the Holy Spirit. I have seen that many live a life of "me and my family only" when we have a lot of people whose lives we could have affected positively with the word, if we were ready to release their strength for the work of God. This is where we are supposed to invest our God-given strength.

People often look for what they had, but could not find any more, or what they know will add value to their lives. Men, for instance, are often busy looking for the woman who they think will suit them because of what they believe they lack. I myself felt I needed a woman with wisdom to manage the home (Proverbs 14:1). I needed a woman who would supplement my weakness, and I went looking for one. Some men would marry a woman for her height. Very emotional men, like me, want a woman who will be there to make them happy, to feel cared for and appreciated as they are. Some don't have a choice, and would marry any woman they see, because they don't have a vision to drive.

Those who drive visions will want a helpmeet from God. There are many women whom men admire, even wishing their husbands dead so that they can start flirting with them. What do women look for in a man? They want protection, care, love and shelter. Every woman desires her own kitchen. Women may not necessarily marry for good looks or money, but they desire these more than life, because they want to be seen outside and appreciated.

To many women, their husband is where that strength lies.

We all need strength to achieve our successes in life, and from what I have said above, the strength I seek may not be what you seek, but in any case, ensure that you seek and find the strength that will take away your weaknesses.

The less your weaknesses, the more you will succeed. And we all need wisdom to search for the strength that will turn our lives into that of the Man God Made. I have also found out that those who are fearfully and beautifully made are filled with wisdom. The ugly, like Goliath, are always filling their thoughts with anger, and as such they lack wisdom. The only way ugly people get attention is through rebellion, so that people will notice and listen to them. So ugly people are mostly filled with demonic illusions. If I need advice, I often go after those who are fearfully and wonderfully made. These sets of people are exposed because of their nature, and they have a lot of wisdom. The ugly hide from people, and they lack, in most cases, the right knowledge and understanding of the true nature of things. They like to be easily noticed, and they will cause chaos once they are given an opportunity, because they will not want their advice to hit the wall. The term ugly, as used above, refers to those who have their dwelling with the devil. They have a heart of stone: an unforgiving and unrepentant heart.

The security forces go after sophisticated weapons and the defensive training they had is the strength they need to succeed. The Bible refers to them as trusting in their chariots.

If we will tell ourselves the truth, which is bitter, we should set our eyes on the elements of life that can give us the strength which will improve our lives, spiritually and physically. This is where the word of God comes in. Apostle John was told by the Angel of God in Revelation 10:8-11 to eat the word of God as food, and it was sweet in his mouth but became bitter in his stomach, because the word is the truth - and the truth is bitter:

And the voice which I heard from Heaven spake unto me again, and said, Go and take the little book which is open in the hand of the angel which standeth upon the sea and upon the Earth. And I went unto the angel, and said unto him, Give me the little book. And he said unto me, Take it, and eat it up; and it shall make thy belly bitter, but it shall be in thy mouth sweet as honey. And I took the little book out of the angel's hand, and ate it up; and it was in my mouth sweet as honey: and as soon as I had eaten it, my belly was bitter. And he said unto me, Thou must prophesy again before many peoples, and nations, and tongues, and kings. - Revelation 10:8-11

That little book is the strength he needed to carry on. When we receive strength we should use it to do the work of God. The reason for the bitterness he had in his stomach is found in Luke 24:32: They asked each other, *"Were not our hearts burning within us while he talked with us on the road and opened the Scriptures to us?" The word of God purges us of dead works, and makes our face shine before God.*

To the lazy, everything is hard and they don't want to seek God, who will reveal hidden secrets to them to help them achieve their desires in life. They want to clap hands in the church and walk away, waiting for someone to feed them and clothe them, or they would prefer to steal to live. This is what I call the act of socio-spiritual dehumanization.

Every spiritual secret that is meant to draw them closer to God is a hard saying to the lazy – see John 6:56-63, below:

He that eateth my flesh, and drinketh my blood, dwelleth in me, and I in him. As the living Father hath sent me, and I live by the Father: so he that eateth me, even he shall live by me. This is that bread which came down from Heaven: not as your fathers did eat manna, and are dead: he that eateth of this bread shall live forever. These things said he in the synagogue, as he taught in Capernaum. Many therefore of his disciples, when they had heard this, said, This is an hard saying; who can hear it? When Jesus knew in himself that his disciples murmured at it, he said unto them, Doth this offend you? What and if ye shall see the Son of man ascend up where he was before? It is the spirit that quickeneth; the flesh profiteth nothing: the words that I speak unto you, they are spirit, and they are life.

Verse 56 talks of how we can receive spiritual strength. And later in John 6:66, those He ministered to abandoned Him for their own pleasure. For us to receive the strength that will sustain us in life, I will use the word of Jesus above: It is the spirit that quickeneth; the flesh profiteth nothing: the words that I speak unto you, they are spirit, and they are life. Anyone without the spirit of God will never succeed in life. From the context above, strength can be seen to come through:

1. Digesting the word of God.
2. Fellowship with Christ in the spirit.
3. Taking the communion.

Strength is measured in the spiritual, through our spiritual maturity, and in the physical through how wealthy and healthy we are (3 John 1:2). The Bible says: *The blessings of the Lord maketh rich.* Richness is measured in spiritual maturity, wealth and health. Once we fail spiritually, we become poor in health and wealth. God gives us strength to live in the spirit, seek wealth and live a healthy life.

We now need to summarise what we need to receive the strength we may have been searching for. The blessing of the Lord is the strength you desire, and the Bible says in Isaiah 30:15: *For thus saith the Lord GOD, the Holy One of Israel; In returning and rest shall ye be saved; in quietness and in confidence shall be your strength: ...*

To be saved, we need to RETURN to God and depend on Him as our REST.

To build strength to carry on after we have repented, we need to be QUIET (also seen in Ecclesiastes 5:2), so that we can study the word of God, and listen to what we are taught by our teachers whom God has raised (Jeremiah 3:15), whom you are also supposed to see and know (Isaiah 30:20). In doing this, we build CONFIDENCE in God (Hebrew 11:6).

Meditation, thinking, and hopeful living are the display of the confidence you have in God.

How does confidence come? *1 John 3:18-22 gives the answer: My little children, let us not love in word, neither in tongue; but in deed and in truth. And hereby we know that we are of the truth, and shall assure our hearts before him. For if our heart condemn us, God is greater than our heart, and knoweth all things. Beloved, if our heart condemn us not, then have we confidence toward God. And whatsoever we ask, we receive of him, because we keep his commandments, and do those things that are pleasing in his sight.*

When we receive the word of God into us, and we are not guilty in our hearts, it shows that we have the confidence of already having been saved. But, if we are still going to be frightened of perishing in eternal hell whenever we hear the word of God, we should repent now. It is only when you have this confidence and the assurance of Heaven that your feet will become beautiful. The Bible says in Isaiah 52:7: *How beautiful upon the mountains are the feet of him that bringeth good tidings, that publisheth peace; that bringeth good tidings of good, that publisheth salvation; that saith unto Zion, Thy God reigneth!*

If you want your feet to be beautiful and appreciated, just

obey the commandments of God. You don't need to meet a prophet to anoint your feet. If we do the will of God, we don't need anyone to anoint our feet for favour. All beautiful feet receive honour from people, as one who had been treated with honour and respect. And the Bible says that the only way to have beautiful feet is to preach the word of God, as we just read in Isaiah 52:7 above.

Now, you are going to meet obstacles on your way as you go forth to do the work of God. This is where you need the strength of God to help you carry on. After he had eaten the scroll, in Ezekiel 3:1-3, God encouraged Ezekiel with these words, in Ezekiel 3:5-7: *For thou art not sent to a people of a strange speech and of an hard language, but to the house of Israel; Not to many people of a strange speech and of an hard language, whose words thou canst not understand. Surely, had I sent thee to them, they would have hearkened unto thee. But the house of Israel will not hearken unto thee; for they will not hearken unto me: for all the house of Israel are impudent and hardhearted.*

Anyone who is born of God overcomes the world. Here is where our faith comes in, 1 John 5:3-5.

Another way to receive strength is through the anointing of God, mostly as a chosen vessel from the womb: *Then the word of the LORD came unto me, saying, Before I formed thee in the belly I knew thee; and before thou camest forth out of the womb I sanctified thee, and I ordained thee a prophet unto the nations.* - *Jeremiah 1:3*

Our talents are God's gifts in our lives and should bring God's favour to us.

Again, we can also receive strength through subordination. When you are submissive under someone whom God has equipped with the strength to succeed, learning under such a person will equip you for success. This is where humility comes into play. And to be humble, you need the Holy Spirit. We can see this in Jesus to us, Elijah to Elisha, and Moses to Joshua. In the world, this is the easiest way to receive physical strength – the knowledge to do your work successfully. Academic pursuit also qualifies as physical strength in this regard.

Now let's take a look at some of the figures in the Bible:

Joshua

Joshua had to lead the children of God against all odds. Denying himself the pleasures of life, he and Caleb had to stake their lives against the murmuring crowd of Israel. Joshua was courageous in the midst of a rebellious generation.

King David

He was bold enough to confront the wild animals that came to eat his father's herd. This boldness is what made him also confront Goliath. So we can say that strength is the bedrock of boldness. You cannot be bold until you are sure that the power in you can confront the obstacle ahead of you. David thereafter fought wars to ensure that the enemy did not enslave God's children.

Samson

Samson had to wear Nazarene hair throughout his childhood until he was an adult and was led astray. Strength is not easy to come by when you don't have Christ in you. But we must leave something for the sake of God. Samson's hair was not to be touched. Samson was a judge who stood as God's armour of war against the Philistines.

This was a mark of covenant. Abraham had to circumcise all male children in his household to enable them to walk with God. This is how strength comes.

As I said earlier, if it had not been for the sin of Adam, his children would not have had the need to sacrifice unto God. We are looking for God for strength today because we are not on good terms with Him. In the same way, the Ten Commandments wouldn't have been necessary if the children of Israel had not murmured against God in Exodus 15:24, but obeyed God's instruction to Moses in Exodus 3:12. Jesus says that if we love God and do His command, then the Godhead will live in us. This is the fact explained in 1 Kings 2:2-3, below:

I go the way of all the Earth: be thou strong therefore, and shew thyself a man; And keep the charge of the Lord thy God, to walk in his ways, to keep his statutes, and his commandments, and his judgments, and his testimonies, as it is written in the law of Moses, that thou mayest prosper in all that thou doest, and withersoever thou turnest thyself; - 1 Kings 2:2, 3

To minister to the world the way the apostles did could only be achieved by a man of strength. In the Bible extract above, it is clear that we all need strength to be regarded as the creation of God. Have you ever wondered how the animals stay in the forest in the midst of both human and animal predators, which come to hunt them for food? How they cope in adverse weather conditions? What about the effects of pollution on them? If animals can survive all these, we should stop complaining and rather ask ourselves how we can showcase the strength God gave to us the day man was made. If there was no strength in Adam, God wouldn't rely on his judgement to name all the animals, or his ability to subdue the Earth. Where is your strength? Are you allowing events to weigh you down?

Some believers would say the Bible says: by strength shall no man prevail, and as such they can sleep all day long to live as pests on others. "Prevail" as used in that Biblical context is spiritual defence. Adam lived in that garden alone, naming all the beasts of the Earth. No one can fathom the extent of this strength that God endowed Adam with. Enormous strength would be the right word.

Man lives a life of dual responsibility, physical and spiritual. Once we can prevail in the spiritual, we become successful in the physical. Here we need to fast, pray and wait on the Lord. Lazy people cannot achieve this. Fasting and praying is not for lazy people. The lazy are made for the day, they don't think of a future.

If physical strength was not needed, there will be no need praying for the spirit of might to come upon us (Isaiah 11:2). Strength gives you the stamina to think, to carry on against all oppositions, to defend your territory against intruders, to wait patiently on the Lord, to minister the gospel, to write books, to continue working till you are retired, etc. This is the kind of strength we all need to live as the Man God Made.

For us to have a full understanding of this term, we need to take a look at what Saint Paul said in 1 Corinthians 9:24-25: *Know ye not that they which run in a race run all, but one receiveth the prize? So run, that ye may obtain. And every man that striveth for the mastery is temperate in all things.*

We all need strength to complete whatsoever duty God has called us to do here on Earth. The beginning of verse 25 above says that the only way to become successful in the application of the strength God has given to us is by being temperate. This also points to our ability to be patient in whatsoever we do. This way we will not be easily worn out. This is where seeking wisdom from God comes in; else we will be parked halfway to our destination.

The Man God Made is full of strength which makes him spirit filled, bold as a lion, temperate in all things, grazing for more grace, dedicated to the work of God and focused on his calling. We would see below what the God kind of strength in us can do. And here I will be personifying strength to make us know that strength is a living being in us.

1. He enables us to defend our faith

The book of 1 Timothy 6:12 says *Fight the good fight of faith, lay hold on eternal life.*

Defending your faith is a good fight. Serving God without the Holy Spirit empowering us is like someone who is on his way to the Moon without a mission and a return date. Since we know that there is an enemy of God called Satan, who will hunt us daily, we must be equipped to defend what we believe. Jesus says this process is a forceful one (Matthew 11:12). Obeying God is all that can help us to succeed.

Awake, awake; put on thy strength, O Zion; put on thy beautiful garments, O Jerusalem, the holy city: for henceforth there shall no more come into thee the uncircumcised and the unclean. Shake thyself from the dust; arise, and sit down, O Jerusalem: loose thyself from the bands of thy neck, O captive daughter of Zion. For thus saith the LORD, Ye have sold yourselves for nought; and ye shall be redeemed without money. Isaiah 52:1-3

2. He enables us to provide for our families

Again the book of 1 Timothy 5:8 says: *But if any provide not for his own, and especially for those of his own house, he hath denied the faith, and is worse than an infidel.*

Here we are told that our inability to provide for our families shows that we are not of God, because we have denied the faith. And denying the faith means denying God (Hebrew 11:6). The book of Proverbs 31:10-31 talks of how the virtuous woman makes provision for her household.

So many women will quickly blame their husbands, for instance, for not been able to provide for the family, and would ignore their own share of the responsibility. The term used above is a requirement for the Man God Made, which Genesis 1:26 refers to as "them" and verse 27 refers to "them" as male and female. We should think daily about our own responsibility to ensure that the family grows into a strong household of God. Over time, I have noticed that families who lack food, shelter, and clothing hardly find anything good in their service to God.

They often become the burden of the local church, who they see should provide these for them. While this happens, gradually, the main focus of teaching the word is diminished into that of Warfare, Welfare and Materialism (WWM). This is why in Acts 6:1-4, the disciples said:

And in those days, when the number of the disciples was multiplied, there arose a murmuring of the Grecians against the Hebrews, because their widows were neglected in the daily ministration. Then the twelve called the multitude of the disciples unto them, and said, It is not reason that we should leave the word of God, and serve tables. Wherefore, brethren, look ye out among you seven men of honest report, full of the Holy Ghost and wisdom, whom we may appoint over this business. But we will give ourselves continually to prayer, and to the ministry of the word.

This is why I also quarrel with those who have children without thinking of how they are going to cater for them. It is a sin to disgrace God in public, because our families could not be catered for, as the image and likeness of God.

3. He enables us to preach the gospel

Once the Disciples were empowered from above with the Holy Spirit, they became bold (Acts 2). Jesus referred to this kind of strength in Acts 1:8 as "power." They got the kind of power that is still working wonders in the world until now, the moment the Holy Spirit came upon them. The strength of God in us enables us to build a God-fearing society.

4. He enables us to lead effectively

Leadership is hinged on our relationship with God. We are like a door, while the plan and purpose of God are the frame and our righteousness is the hinges upon which we turn. Whereas the knowledge and understanding of God we have is like the latch. The wisdom of God in us, which we received through asking from Him, is the handle, and the key that locks the door to the frame so that there is a perfect seal between the door and the frame. The wall where the frame is fixed is God. The only thing that will unlock this door to ensure that we are not totally in God's plan and purpose is sin. If we are not living in sin, then we can lead others effectively, because we are firmly united with God.

5. He enables us to follow effectively

This is the same as what we just discussed. As long as we are not cast out of God's presence because of sins, we will also be able to follow leaders effectively. This is possible because God also reveals His plans to us, even as we follow our leaders. Once we are disconnected from God, we will certainly rebel, because we will find it difficult to trust the decisions of our leaders.

We need to renew our strength from time to time through our desire to renew our relationship with God in our confession of our sins, and return to God – 1 John 1. We will now discuss what we need to walk in the strength God has ordained for us:

1. Knowledge seeking

This is where many of us go wrong. We have, over the years, sought after only the wrong knowledge, which is now taking us far from God. The internet, with its plethora of information, gives us a proof of what sort of knowledge people seek daily. Human minds think in diverse ways, and we often yield to the devil's insinuated negative information rather than godly information. Every day I study the word of God, I become more informed of the reason for God's declaration in Hosea 4:6: *My people are destroyed for lack of knowledge…* Then as now, man's insatiability would not allow him to settle down to think about the reason for what now exists on Earth.

The book of 1 John 1:1 says: *That which was from the beginning, which we have heard, which we have seen with our eyes, which we have looked upon.*

Why can't we sit down and think about them? This is knowledge seeking. There is nothing new under the sun. All we know today and have yet to know has existed from the beginning. It is our duty to seek the right knowledge which will make us acceptable before God. And in the verse we just read, we can see that there are two avenues in which we can become informed: *hearing and seeing.* Then we create the image of what we heard and saw in our thoughts, through repetitive consideration of the most pronounced message in what we heard or saw. This is the process simply explained in that 1 John 1:1, as "looked upon." It is the act of "looking upon" that made Eve respond to temptation (Genesis 3:6). So the act of knowledge seeking is more than just coming across information; *it involves continuous listening through teaching, continuous seeing through study and the act of thoughtful consideration, which is often referred to as meditation.*

2. Seeking understanding

Without understanding in all information that comes our way, the knowledge we receive is useless. 1 John 1:1 ends with this: *… and our hands have handled, of the Word of life.* It is how much of the information you can handle that makes you who you are. To have a full grasp of the information before us we must have handled every byte, translating into millions of terabytes what is contained in the knowledge gained. This is what we often refer to as leaving no stone unturned. What is the knowledge that will turn our lives around? The last phrase in 1 John 1:1 says: "of the Word of life". The use of the term "of" before "the word of life" connotes a reference to a subject of importance, or firsthand priority. Our knowledge should therefore reside in the word of God. Whatever we are going to achieve must have its root in the word of God. In verse 4, John says: *And these things write we unto you, that your joy may be full.* The word is the joy you need to excel in life. Understanding is what powers us with all we need to exercise the knowledge that resides in us. This is what John refers to in 1 John 2:5 when the Bible says:

But whoso keepeth His word, in him verily is the love of God perfected: hereby know we that we are in Him.

The moment you are in Him, you become the Man God Made. What poverty does to our minds is to block our receptive senses: see, hear, feel, taste and smell. And as such we end up disagreeing with the word that would help us grow in wisdom, and in the thoughtful application of wisdom.

3. Seeking Wisdom

Wisdom simply refers to the domain of wise knowledge and understanding. This domain is inhabited by both humans and spirits. We hear God's wisdom when we are within His domain of influence. We are told of how Adam and his wife Eve left God's presence, and Cain was brought up with the wrong kind of wisdom (Jeremiah 8:9). And Cain too had to disobey God. He murdered his own brother and later departed from the presence of God. In God's presence, there is fullness of joy. This fullness of joy is what Proverbs refers to below:

Length of days is in her [wisdom's] right hand; and in her left hand riches and honour. - Proverbs 3:16

So, those who seek after the wisdom of God are those who fear God so that God will fulfil their days on Earth. Those who are called by God hear God speaks and are united with His purpose on Earth. These are those who qualify as the Man God Made.

4. Meditation

While I was growing up, I used to think that those who meditate were members of the occult, until I knew its meaning. Isaiah 30:15 is a verse that is often referred to here: in quietness and confidence, the prophet had said while informing us what God requires of us. Meditation is like the regurgitating actions of herbivores. Herbivorous animals would go on and on grazing and would later sit down in the shade to chew their cud. The idiomatic expression "chewing the cud" has come to mean meditating or pondering. Borrowing a leaf from them, we would mean that we need to study the word of God as if we are chewing it and absorbing such a large amount of information, until we can go to a quiet place where we can sit all day or night to have a deep and a thoughtful review of all the information we had gathered. Then we would filter it and align it to our vision and aspirations on Earth, in line with God's plan for us.

5. Building Confidence

This is how faith grows. If we can build our confidence in God we will see increase in all that we do. Many would trust in their Earthly wisdom, their certificates and relationships with people as a yardstick to success, and here is where they fail.

6. Loving our neighbours

This will help reduce those who will make you lose focus by the way they act towards you. When you live in an unfriendly environment, you will become unstable spiritually, as you have to continually keep watch on the acts of the enemy, and in that way, your productive time will reduce. The only way to overcome the pestering faces of hatred from people is to show them heartfelt love. Let your love extend beyond the boundary of the carnal world.

7. Loving God

This is the foundation of all that we have been discussing. This is self-explanatory. If we would love God, He will fight the enemy on our behalf so that we are not taken out of His presence by sin.

CHAPTER SEVEN

MAN MADE MALE AND FEMALE

This is where Adam failed. He didn't recognise that without Eve by his side, there was no way he could succeed. Hence he quickly blamed Eve, in the hope that he would be exonerated from the wrath of God. I don't agree that people should not be married. Marriage is a perfectly ordained institution of God to enable the blessings upon the man to take effect. Proverbs 18:22 says: *Whoso findeth a wife findeth a good thing, and obtaineth favour of the LORD.*

Not favour "from" the Lord, but "of" the Lord, because it is an established spiritual order, right from the foundation of the world. The New King James Version replaced the word, "of" with "from", changing the original meaning of that verse.

The use of the term "of the Lord" shows that this favour is already in existence, but a man needs his wife as a trigger to release this favour, which came into being the day the Lamb was slain from the foundation of the world (Revelations 13:8). If marriage was not important, God wouldn't wait until Mary was betrothed before she was conceived of the Holy Spirit.

This entity of unity, male and female, is whom God blessed, and not to operate independently. To build Heavenly children, we must build a virile family and ensure that the family altar is strong, so as to lead every member of that household to God. And instead of our mothers, wives and daughters seeing themselves as the weaker sex, they should now know that society is suffering because they have decided to behave like Eve, who preferred to dine with Satan, through gossip, and the display of lukewarm attitudes.

The Man God Made is a complete entity of wisdom, knowledge and understanding. Now that they are separated as physical individual entity, not until both live as one spiritual entity will the purpose of God for the Man God Made be fulfilled.

A pastor's wife is also a pastor, judging from Paul's argument in 1 Corinthians 9:5. No argument about this. God would not call a man without his wife being part of the calling. There is something I saw in the circumcision that Zipporah, the wife of Moses, performed on their son to save Moses' life. A whole nation would have been unsaved if Moses had died (Exodus 4:18-26). She was the real arm that God used to save the Israelites, and later her father also came to give Moses the counsel that alleviated his pains of leadership. Miriam, his sister, had also saved his life as a baby.

There is something I also discovered while growing up; the

children of the loved woman in a polygamous home were always given attention by their father, the way it happened to Joseph and Benjamin, in Jacob and Rachael's case. And, again, children who have a mother filled with godly wisdom will always succeed in life; we can see this in Jacob's life, for his mother, Rebecca, knew how to seek the face of God. Mary, the mother of Jesus, was all about Jesus even to His point of death.

In Jeremiah 1:4-5, God says that He formed, sanctified and anointed Jeremiah in his mother's womb, meaning that God and the host of Heaven were present in the womb, to ensure Jeremiah was wonderfully and fearfully made. And in the case of Jesus, the Holy Spirit resided in Mary's womb for nine months, making her more of a holy mountain of God throughout this period of nine months. Every womb that bore God's anointed is Holy unto God, and as such, every woman who gives birth to a servant of God is favoured of God to be a bearer of the touch of salvation. Many women lack the wisdom of God to stand firm and their houses are devoid of God's help and presence (Nahum 2:13, Proverbs 14:1).

We will get acquainted with the duties of the male and that of the female as we read on, and we will see how this holistically represents the intention of God for the Man God Made.

And he answered and said unto them, Have ye not read, that he which made them at the beginning made them male and female, and said, For this cause shall a man leave father and mother, and shall cleave to his wife: and they twain shall be one flesh? - Matthew 19:4-5

In the Bible, right from the book of Leviticus, women were treated as weaker sexes. This gave woman a false image as someone inferior to their male counterpart. Many feel that the Bible preaches against women's authority to preach the word of God, especially in the pulpit. I am called by God, and God never told me to treat women as such. I believe that the proponents of the doctrine against women preachers are speaking against those women who are yet to be saved (1 Corinthians 9:5). If this is the case, then it also applies to men who are also yet to be saved. In our church, the same standard of choice of who stands before the congregation to represent Christ is made by God.

When I was quickened to anoint my wife to serve in the Lord's vineyard, I was hesitant in doing so until I was convinced in my spirit that without her there by my side, there was no way I would become the Man God Made. The following verses confirm this judgement that the woman is no less than the man:

Galatians 3:28: There is neither Jew nor Greek, slave nor free, male nor female, for you are all one in Christ Jesus.

Genesis 1:26 - 27: Then God said, "Let us make man in our image, in our likeness"...So God created man in His own image, in the image of God He created him; male and female He created them.

Genesis 2:18: The Lord God said "It is not good for the man to be alone. I will make a helper suitable for him.

Genesis 2:23: The man said, "This is now bone of my bones and flesh of my flesh; she shall be called 'woman', for she was taken out of man.

They were to complement one another. There is no such thing as "the man reigns supreme", except after the curse upon Eve: *...and thy desire shall be to thy husband, and he shall rule over thee - Genesis 3:16.*

The program *Snapped*, on DSTV's Criminal and Investigation Network Channel, aired in 2011, does not represent the woman God presented to Adam. The makers of the programme claimed that it is a true crime documentary television series produced by Jupiter Entertainment which features the stories of real women who killed others, mainly husbands or boyfriends. God wouldn't make such mistakes, to give Adam a help that would mar his life. The devil is the one who does that mutilation on women, the way he deceived Eve in the garden. Today many unrepentant women still wants their husbands dead.

At the upper room, in the book of Acts chapter 2, the women who were with the disciples equally received the Holy Spirit and they were to obey the voice of Jesus in Acts 1:8; failure to do so would be an act of treason felony against Jesus.

Acts 1:8: But ye shall receive power, after that the Holy Ghost is come upon you: and ye shall be witnesses unto me both in Jerusalem, and in all Judaea, and in Samaria, and unto the uttermost part of the Earth.

Acts 1:12-14: Then returned they unto Jerusalem from the mount called Olivet, which is from Jerusalem a sabbath day's journey. And when they were come in, they went up into an upper room, where abode both Peter, and James, and John, and Andrew, Philip, and Thomas, Bartholomew, and Matthew, James the son of Alphaeus, and Simon Zelotes, and Judas the brother of James. These all continued with one accord in prayer and supplication, with the women, and Mary the mother of Jesus, and with his brethren.

Acts 2:1-4: And when the day of Pentecost was fully come, they were all with one accord in one place. And suddenly there came a sound from Heaven as of a rushing mighty wind, and it filled all the house where they were sitting. And there appeared unto them cloven tongues like as of fire, and it sat upon each of them. And they were all filled with the Holy Ghost, and began to speak with other tongues, as the Spirit gave them utterance.

They were all together in one accord, meaning there was no discrimination. They all spoke in tongues, meaning God never discriminated against the woman. So, what is all the argument about? A saved woman is as important to God as a saved man. In the same way, an unsaved woman wants God to save her as much as an unsaved man.

Male and female He created them. This is the most perfect

combination of a purpose-driven destiny. Charity begins at home, they say. God created the male and female sexes to enable mankind to enjoy the blessings of a relationship and practise the culture of good neighbourliness. As they live, they are entrusted with the Holy Spirit to enable them to build trust, intimacy and mutual dependency in love.

I strongly believe that the disunity we see today is the devil's initial plan to punish man, before he found his way into that garden in line with Revelation 12:12. Once the bond of unity was broken, Adam started to blame his wife, who he earlier confessed was his bone and flesh, who was supposed to be his lifetime companion. This was exactly what the devil wanted to happen in Heaven until he was cast down to Earth.

With the curse of God upon them, separate positions of authority also exist, with an altered line of reporting from what God originally established in place, and the support the man was to get from the woman greatly diminished. Although this however, does not separate them physically. They still had to bear children whom they had to raise together. They still had to sleep together to provide warmth for each other. They still had to talk together to prevent the devil from taking hold of them, as they now lived outside the presence of God.

This is not an indication of the woman being less

important, nor is it a licence to abuse her position as a co-pilot in the affairs in the home, society or in the church.

In marriage, a unique 'being' comes into existence who is supposed to be a replica of the Man God Made: the image and likeness of God. The Bible sees them as 'one flesh':

...a man will leave his father and mother and be united to his wife, and they will become one flesh. - Genesis 2:24

To regain the status of this 'one flesh,' every couple must relate together in sexual union; a relationship that should create warmth, spiritually and emotionally. This way they will be able to share their strengths and their weaknesses together.

A loving sexual relationship between a man and a woman should be a combination of reciprocated confidence founded on trust and inter-dependence. Any act of violation of the marriage union, whether sexual, emotional or spiritual, will have a negative effect on the purpose of the 'one flesh' proclamation from God. Infidelity is the aftermath of an emotionally broken marriage: it is the result of the lack of submission. The Bible deals with this specially, in Ephesians 5:22-30:

Wives, submit yourselves unto your own husbands, as unto the Lord. For the husband is the head of the wife, even as Christ is the head of the church: and he is the saviour of the body. Therefore as the church is subject unto Christ, so let the wives be to their own husbands in everything. Husbands, love your wives, even as Christ also loved the church, and gave himself for it; That he might sanctify and cleanse it with the washing of water by the word, That he might present it to himself a glorious church, not having spot, or wrinkle, or any such thing; but that it should be holy and without blemish. So ought men to love their wives as their own bodies. He that loveth his wife loveth himself. For no man ever yet hated his own flesh; but nourisheth and cherisheth it, even as the Lord the church: For we are members of his body, of his flesh, and of his bones.

SYMBOLIC REPRESENTATION OF MARRIAGE

Our understanding of the mystery of the marriage submission requirement will enable us to love God the more. God created marriage to represent the union between Christ and His Church.

Matthew 25:1, 10: At that time the kingdom of Heaven will be like ten virgins who took their lamps and went out to meet the bridegroom... the virgins who were ready went in with Him to the wedding banquet, and the door was shut.

Revelation 19:7: Let us rejoice and be glad and give Him glory! For the wedding of the Lamb has come, and His bride has made herself ready.

Here, the church must therefore, make a frantic effort to seek God and do His will. After doing His will, the church will now receive special beautification from God as seen below:

Revelation 21:2: I saw the Holy City, the new Jerusalem [the Church], coming down out of Heaven from God, prepared as a bride beautifully dressed for her husband.

Marriage is more important to God than it is to us. We can't exist independently of each other. In one accord, we would break bread together and propagate the gospel of Christ unto the end of the world.

CHAPTER EIGHT

MAN MADE UNIQUE

Our thumbprints show that we are indeed unique individuals. Science has proven that no two persons have the same thumbprint. Isn't God wonderful? Before the Man God Made, there was none that was made in the same image and likeness of God. Every other creation of the Earth was generated from lifelessness – the Earth and the sky. But man was created from life. This made him unique. This unique nature may be connected with the reason the serpent couldn't exist without them. This uniqueness is seen in the prophecy that announced the coming of the Messiah:

Therefore the Lord himself shall give you a sign; Behold, a virgin shall conceive, and bear a son, and shall call his name Immanuel.
- Isaiah 7:14

As we read earlier, the serpent must have been a regular visitor who just stayed to watch the paradise that man was living in. What then is the essence of being unique? We can also see this evidence in the lives of those called by God in the Bible.

We will be discussing this from what we know makes up the human being: spiritually (deity), psychologically (mental coordination, mind, thought), physiologically (form), sociologically (power of association), and biologically (the human brain).

Spiritual Perspective

First the very creation of man points to one fact, which is that he will live to submit under the authority of his creator, God, who is a spirit. Jesus came to let us know that the missing link between us and God is connected with the fact that we have neglected our existence as spiritual beings, and as such we can hardly communicate with our God. John 4:23-24:

23 But the time is come [But the hour cometh], and now it is, when true worshippers shall worship the Father in spirit and truth; for also the Father seeketh such, that worship him.

24 God is a Spirit, and it behooveth them that worship him, to worship in spirit and truth. (Wycliffe Bible translation).

I decided to use the Wycliffe Bible because of the word "behooveth" in verse 24. The word "behoove" means: "to be necessary, proper, or advantageous for..." (Merriam-Webster dictionary). It is proper for us, and it is to our advantage that we reverence God in the Spirit. This is only when we can receive from God.

Psychological Perspective

We are told to love God with all our heart, mind and soul. These terms are holistic psychological terms. Psychology deals with mental coordination, or what I will refer to as spiritual balance. Psychologists have studied the minds and behaviours of people and societies based on the actions they see us carry out. The Bible says that what we do is directly linked to what kind of information we sow in our hearts (Luke 6:45). It is not uncommon to see children born of the same parents and raised up in the same home acting differently. This is the element of uniqueness in each of us. Twelve disciples studied and lived with Jesus, yet one of them was a devil (John 6:70).

Physiological Perspective

Closely related to anatomy, which is the study of the framework of the human body, physiology is the study of the function of each of the parts and organs that make up the body. Why is this study important to the creation of man? We can take a close look into this in Genesis 1:26, where God made man, whom He later called "male and female." We can see that structurally the male and the female are different, and as such the difference in their structure also creates the difference we see in the function of their respective organs and their physical outlook, thinking, behaviours and preferences in life.

The healing miracles we see are directed into making these unique elements of the human physiological body to be in the form and likeness in which, God made them from the day that man was made.

Sociological Perspective

This is somewhat connected with our discussion above. Humans interact with their environments to try to understand God better. Social interactions usually gives birth to the existence of both barbaric and civilized living patterns. In all, we are able to isolate a godly behaviour from an ungodly one. Even within the godly, we have classified people as churchgoers, believers, born-again, social Christians, etc. These are the results of people interpreting the Bible to suit their beliefs, which may have root in the social lives that they exist in. Will God ever accept these classifications? Never! We are either for Him or against Him. Repentance is the right word here, and we should not cut corners in order to defend our ill-thought lives.

Biological Perspective

Biology is the study of plants and animals. And in the study of animals, human beings are included. To me this is derogatory. The Bible told us that plants and animals came to exist out of the environment that will finally become their habitat, but God created man in His image and likeness.

Biology should therefore be seen as the study of plants, animals and human beings.

Biology is a science, because it involves the use of empirical evidence to establish a fact that can be proven and will apply anywhere, provided the same empirical study steps are adopted. My major concern here is the human brain, and what biology has to offer about the uniqueness of the human brain. It is fascinating to know that every action we carry out is controlled by our brain. The brain is located in a place where it faces Heaven, almost all the time. What then makes the human brain unique, and different from that of other creatures? The fact that we are formed by God, and God commanded us to have dominion over whatever He had created before man, shows that the human brain, which coordinates all that we do, must be capable of handling the responsibilities of dominion. This can be proven by the different languages that we hear and speak.

An early proof of this is how Adam was able to name all the living creatures that God brought to him, and remember their names thereafter. To me, for God to respect the judgement of the Man God Made shows that his brain is a God-kind of brain.

Jesus says that anyone who sees Him likewise sees God (John 14:7), which is only possible when we have a pure heart, diffused in the likeness of God.

We will now see what all these translate to: The first is human talents, or gifts. What are gifts? What are talents? These are what people will usually see in us, and they often become the point of attraction. Many of us have failed in life because our gifts are not a true reflection of what God anointed us with from the womb. And, as such, we are not living as unique individuals. We can recognise our individual gifts when we submit ourselves in God's plan (Exodus 31:1-11). And to do this we need wisdom, which is the manifestation of both knowledge and understanding.

The wisdom residing in us shows that the way and manner in which we understand the knowledge we gain varies: craftsmanship, handwriting skill, our thumbprints, voices, etc, depend on our unique abilities.

For David to be after the heart of God shows that he was indeed unique. What then are the elements of someone who is unique? Some are listed below:

1. They don't envy others, because they are above their unbelieving peers and are not into a competition with anybody (Deuteronomy 28:13). They are Heaven driven (Matthew 6:20), and these are the ones who see their Earthly achievements as instruments for evangelism and sustaining peace in society, because they have the covenant of peace living in their hearts: *Let us not be desirous of vain glory, provoking one another, envying one another. Galatians 5:26.*

I have manifested thy name unto the men which thou gavest me out of the world: thine they were, and thou gavest them me; and they have kept thy word. Sanctify them through thy truth: thy word is truth. John 17:6,17.

2. They are formed, sanctified and ordained by God: *Before I formed thee in the belly I knew thee; and before thou camest forth out of the womb I sanctified thee, and I ordained thee a prophet unto the nations. Jeremiah 1:5*

3. They love the things of God: *I beseech you therefore, brethren, by the mercies of God, that ye present your bodies a living sacrifice, holy, acceptable unto God, which is your reasonable service. And be not conformed to this world: but be ye transformed by the renewing of your mind, that ye may prove what is that good, and acceptable, and perfect, will of God. Romans 12:1-2*

4. They lend a helping hand to others: *Withhold not good from them to whom it is due, when it is in the power of thine hand to do it. Proverbs 3:27*

5. They study the word of God to grow: *Study to shew thyself approved unto God, a workman that needeth not to be ashamed, rightly dividing the word of truth. 2 Timothy 2:15*

6. They stay out of sexual sin: *Flee fornication. Every sin that a man doeth is without the body; but he that committeth fornication sinneth against his own body. - 1 Corinthians 6:18.*

7. They do not blaspheme the name of God by mocking the work of God: *But he that shall blaspheme against the Holy Ghost hath never forgiveness, but is in danger of eternal damnation.* - Mark 3:29.

CHAPTER NINE

MAN MADE PERFECT

God saw that the man He had made was good. This is why God continually looked for those who were perfect or who could walk the path of perfection to be used as instruments of restoration. This can be seen in His reference to Noah and Job, and the call of Abraham.

We may be unique and yet not perfect. It is our ability to transform our uniqueness into perfection that makes us a true replica of the Man God Made. This fact is clear from the verse below:

Ecclesiastes 7:29: Lo, this only have I found, that God hath made man upright; but they have sought out many inventions.

What inventions is the above verse referring to? It is referring to our evil ways, which are borne out of our love for evil and deceitful wisdom.

The following discussion explains the quality of what God expects in that man, who was a combined male and female.

1. Job was upright (righteous) and perfect (Job 1:8). This is the hallmark of integrity. As an upright and perfect man,

he saw the need to always intercede on behalf of his children:

And his sons went and feasted in their houses, everyone his day; and sent and called for their three sisters to eat and to drink with them. And it was so, when the days of their feasting were gone about, that Job sent and sanctified them, and rose up early in the morning, and offered burnt offerings according to the number of them all: for Job said, It may be that my sons have sinned, and cursed God in their hearts. Thus did Job continually – Job 1:4-5

His integrity was not shared by his children because his wife was not perfect, and that made the entire household imperfect. This could be seen in his wife's advice to him that he should deface his integrity by cursing God (Job 2:9), even when she knew that he would eventually die when he did so: *Then said his wife unto him, dost thou still retain thine integrity? Curse God, and die.* This is the same with many women today, they have no knowledge of who God is. They are in the church to secure their marriages, because the Bible preaches monogamy. If it were otherwise, they would have preferred witch doctors to help them secure their marriages and to ensure that their children are favoured by their husbands. We need to teach women today about God so that we can have a glorious service as a family unto God.

2. In Genesis 6:8 we are told that Noah found grace in the eyes of the Lord and, as such, he was righteous before God. Noah's rescue mission was aimed at creating a platform for repentance and not necessarily to enable God to harvest the righteous out of the world. It wasn't a time to winnow. Even when Noah was saved, he later, in Genesis 9:25, cursed his grandson. This act of his shows that though he found grace in the eyes of God, he was not perfect. A perfect person would not curse his generation; rather he would intercede on their behalf.

3. Abraham was to walk before God to achieve perfection. He walked with God in faith, but his imperfection can be seen in his inability to seek the face of God when his wife, Sarah offered him Haggai. He lied twice (half lie - half truth), denying his wife because of fear of death (Genesis 12 &20). In one instance, he told Abimelech: *And Abraham said, Because I thought, Surely the fear of God is not in this place; and they will slay me for my wife's sake.*

   If he was perfect he would know how to seek the face of God before embarking on that journey, and God would have revealed to him what would happen to him. A perfect man seeks to look ahead of him all the time, and God would not deny him the truth about the future (Isaiah 42:9).

4. The Ten Commandments would not have been necessary if the children of Israel had had the fear of God in their

hearts. Even Moses broke the original tablet containing the laws inscribed by the finger of God because of anger, and then slaughtered 3000 people that day, those he was supposed to lead into the land of Canaan. This again shows that he wasn't perfect, even though he was humble.

5. Gideon was a man of faith (Hebrew 11:32-33). He delivered God's children from the hands of their oppressors by making himself available for God to use. His imperfection was seen in his inability to choose the kind of men that would go with him to war. At the intervention of God, the 32,000 soldiers he chose were reduced to 300 (Judges 7:1-7). When we are imperfect, we waste resources and end up achieving clumsy targets.

In Matthew 5:48, Jesus made it clear that the Man God Made was made perfect, hence we must return to this perfect order of both spiritual and physical living. The perfect man is a good man. Psalms 37:23 says: *The steps of a good man are ordered by the Lord: and he delighteth in his way.* God would only delight in the ways of an upright and perfect man, as we can see in Job 1:8. To tell us what price we have to pay to become good, Jesus explained in Mark 10:18: *And Jesus said unto him, Why callest thou me good? There is none good but one, that is, God.*

This points to the fact that our steps must be ordered by God to the path of righteousness (Psalms 23:3), and we must walk in this path to become the Man God Made.

Man commits sins because God created the Man God Made with free will. We can renounce evil if we want. For instance in the book of Deuteronomy 30:11-16, Moses expatiated on this fact:

For this commandment which I command thee this day, it is not hidden from thee, neither is it far off. It is not in Heaven, that thou shouldest say, Who shall go up for us to Heaven, and bring it unto us, that we may hear it, and do it? Neither is it beyond the sea, that thou shouldest say, Who shall go over the sea for us, and bring it unto us, that we may hear it, and do it? But the word is very nigh unto thee, in thy mouth, and in thy heart, that thou mayest do it. See, I have set before thee this day life and good, and death and evil; In that I command thee this day to love the LORD thy God, to walk in his ways, and to keep his commandments and his statutes and his judgments, that thou mayest live and multiply: and the LORD thy God shall bless thee in the land whither thou goest to possess it.

We can obey God and do His will if we see the need and chose to do it. And this is the need: that we all need to walk the path of perfection. Our God is everywhere around us, ready to lead us into the path of uprightness and perfection. He is raising shepherds daily according to His promise in Jeremiah 3:15 – to feed you with knowledge and understanding. When pastors slumber, God's children become scattered, and they will lack the right knowledge and understanding to heal their wounds (Nahum 2:18). Keep on searching for that teacher who will lead you to the path of Godliness. You will not search far this day. You don't need to travel kilometres in search for them. Isaiah 30:20-21 says: *And though the Lord give you the bread of adversity, and the water of affliction, yet shall not thy teachers be removed into a corner any more, but thine eyes shall see thy teachers: And thine ears shall hear a word behind thee, saying, This is the way, walk ye in it, when ye turn to the right hand, and when ye turn to the left.*

This is the purpose of God's declaration in Isaiah 42:16: *And I will bring the blind by a way that they knew not; I will lead them in paths that they have not known: I will make darkness light before them, and crooked things straight. These things will I do unto them, and not forsake them.*

Where is God leading us to? Mount Zion! (Isaiah 30:19, Hebrews 12:22). Many of us are the multitudes which dwell in Jerusalem, but God wants those who are separated unto himself, who will dwell in mount Zion. This means that our present day worship arena is likened to Jerusalem, and there we have those who are in mount Zion, who worship God in truth and in spirit. Until we are trained in the wisdom of God, though we are heirs of His Kingdom, we are more like slaves, who have no authority over their inheritance (Galatians 4:1-2). What makes the difference is the approval of God (2 Timothy 2:15).

Your shepherds are all around you, proclaiming Jesus wherever they go, that they may teach you the way of our Lord, to become the approved of God so that you can decree things and they are honoured in your name. In Jesus is the path that leads to your glory. In Him alone, you will find perfection. This is the way, walk therefore in it.

Looking at Deuteronomy 30:11, one would ask: why did Adam choose to disobey God? Was it that God created Adam with an ethical flaw in him which made him defenceless in the midst of temptation? Jesus says that we need to pray so that we do not fall into temptation (Mark 14:38). Was it that Adam never knew how to pray against temptation? Did God ever expect Adam to pray? Was there a need for prayers when there was no sin in place? Can we now live a prayerless life and concentrate on doing the will of God in total obedience to His commands? I still believe that Adam was not having a perfect fellowship with God. Jesus prayed for Himself in John 17, yet He was sinless.

The question comes back again: why on Earth should Adam ever take a decision to dishonour God? This is where imperfection comes in. This is why I am saying that the Man God Made was not the Adam that sinned. That original man, who was, "very good" according to God's approval statement in Genesis 1:31, had a very brief life span – from when he was created, to when God caused a deep sleep to fall on him. Up till the time God took that rib from him, Adam never sinned against God.

When there is no godly leadership in place, chaos is bound to happen as people will do whatsoever pleases them. We can see an example of this happening in Judges 21:25: *In those days there was no king in Israel: every man did that which was right in his own eyes.*

So while Eve may be blamed for the attribute of imperfection we now see in our lives, it is totally untrue that she caused the downfall of man. She too needed someone to talk to, and it was the duty of the husband to direct her to the right source of wisdom (Esther 1:22). But today we can make a change to every form of imperfection in our lives if we can just obey God – not in principle, but in our deeds. Adam responded to the pressure from his wife and that act led him into pain. Are you surrendering to pressures, to disobey God? We can assuage the pressures we experience daily by living like Jesus. To this end, we need to keep on reflecting on the love of God. Keep on reflecting on His mercies and how He delivered you severally from the hands of destruction. It is time to yield, so that we all can become the Man God Made, in perfection.

CHAPTER TEN

MAN MADE CREATIVE

The act of naming all the animals by Adam prior to his downfall shows creativity. To dominate the world requires creativity. Funnily enough, the devil has gone ahead of mankind to divert the heart of man into appreciating evil creative intelligence. Creativity has to do with ingenuity, inspiration, resourcefulness, originality, innovation, etc. Daniel revealed that knowledge will multiply towards the end (Daniel 12:4). We have left the seeking of knowledge to the world instead of being ready to take over challenges with the knowledge of God in us.

I checked my phone call register and I discovered that my outgoing, dialled calls over a two-month period totalled 30 hours 28 minutes 03 seconds and my incoming, received calls registered 5 hours 25 minutes 39 seconds, making a total of 35 hours 53 minutes 41 seconds on the phone in two months. The question now is, what value have these 35-plus hours added to my life? It is time to ask yourself what you do with your phone conversations. For every second you talk, phone companies make money. What have your calls done for you? Have they added value to your life? This is where the sense of creativity starts from.

What then is creativity? Let's look at what happened to Adam after he left the garden.

Modern science has shown that man can create anything; architectural designs are everywhere, worldwide. Man can think anything and create anything. This is not new; the grandsons of Cain invented music, metallurgy and tent building. Abel practiced animal husbandry. Nimrod, for instance, led the building of the tower of Babel, and irrigation was invented in Egypt. Science is about discovery, so we are told. Discovery is born out of the quest for more knowledge. This is an attribute which was inborn in the Man God Made. Do you have the urge for creativity or are you the type who just lives by what others have created?

While animals only react to what their physical senses can appreciate, humans are capable of abstract thinking. The likes of Leonardo da Vinci have created paintings through abstract thinking to depict the events that are happening now hundreds of years ago. While abstract thinking is different from visions and dreams, we are told, in Ecclesiastes 5:3, that a dream is possible when the mind is engaged to think. This means that man's ability to dream is born out of the fact that he has to think, and for those who think abstractly, God will not hold back the future from them (Daniel 2:29). This is the bedrock of intelligent creativity.

Imagination is the fuel that powers our ability to create. When God said "let us make man in our image and likeness", He already knew who the man would be like. This is imagination.

Prayers are born out of realistic imagining. This is what I will term the "Possibility Framework" (PF), because with God all things are possible. If you are not sure that your prayers will be answered, why pray? The whole essence of prayers is to create what was never there, through the promises of God found in the Bible - all the living testimonies of God's handiwork in the Bible, and the testimonies we could see and hear today. This is where we must have the right imagination of what we desire to be in place before we start to pray. My book, How Good and Large Is Your Land? treats this is detail. Now, let's take a look at the book of Matthew 6:9-14:

9 After this manner therefore pray ye: Our Father which art in Heaven, Hallowed be thy name.

10 Thy kingdom come, Thy will be done in Earth, as it is in Heaven.

11 Give us this day our daily bread.

12 And forgive us our debts [trespasses], as we forgive our debtors [trespassers].

13 And lead us not into temptation, but deliver us from evil: For thine is the kingdom, and the power, and the glory, forever. Amen.

14 For if ye forgive men their trespasses, your Heavenly Father will also forgive you

If we read through and through again, you will discover that you will begin to understand the elements of this prayer. The first line says that the father you are talking to lives in Heaven. You must have the right imagination of what Heaven is like, because the right perspective is going to affect the entire prayer. His kingdom must come, and you must recognise His kingdom. His will must be done on Earth, and you must know and do His will. He should forgive you your sins, because you know what forgiveness is all about, and the repercussions of the act of unforgiveness, and so on.

This is creativity. Anyone who lacks the power to create things in his/her mind before the physical manifestation cannot claim to be living in the image and likeness of God. "Let there be" is the language of creativity.

Jesus Christ made us to know that until we believe that what we pray for will be answered, there is no way it can come to pass. This is why we would be judged for every statement that comes from our mouths, because they are creative elements. What we say is what creates the world we see, and the atmosphere we experience around us. And we are also told that we speak what we had sown in our heart (mind).

This is the underlying foundation for faith to exist. See it, say it, dream it, act it and see it established. This is one of the reasons I always feel that, in line with the request of the Disciples, prayers need to be taught, rather than cajoling believers into praying dozens of lines of prayers printed in books. Many don't yet understand what prayers are meant to yield, and they shout and making noise because, to them, God is deaf. Sow the "need" you intend to see in your heart first, and ensure you don't have grudges against any of your brethren, before you talk to God in your closet.

Leonardo da Vinci imagined so many things. Many of them now exist to help mankind, and I would say that his creative power is yet to measure what God created in man. Even so, this is what I got from the online Wikipedia about him:

...an Italian Renaissance polymath: painter, sculptor, architect, musician, scientist, mathematician, engineer, inventor, anatomist, geologist, cartographer, botanist and writer whose genius, perhaps more than that of any other figure, epitomized the Renaissance humanist ideal. Leonardo has often been described as the archetype of the Renaissance Man, a man of "unquenchable curiosity" and "feverishlyinventive imagination".

(http://en.wikipedia.org/wiki/Leonardo_da_Vinci)

If one man could be this creative, what are you doing with

your gift? To me this is the whole essence of being born again: To have the creative mind of God, and put things in order, in order to make life more meaningful. God spoke to Abram in Genesis 12:2: And I will make you a great nation, And I will bless you, And make your name great; And so you shall be a blessing...

You can never be a blessing when you are not creative. This is what God says in Isaiah 43:7:

(Even) every one that is called by my name: for I have created him for my glory, I have formed him; yea, I have made him.

And Matthew 5:16 says that our light must shine to such an extent that God will begin to reap the reward of our exploits, physically and spiritually. How can we shine when we are not creative? If this is the case, we may have been robbing God of His glory already, judging from the book of Isaiah 43:7.

In the sections that follow, we will be discussing what we need to do to become as creative as the Man God Made.

1. See the need for improvement

There is always a way out of that predicament you thought was insurmountable. King Solomon could have decided to suffer like every other person who was sacrificing to other gods, but He resorted to following God and asking Him for wisdom and knowledge (2 Chronicles 1:1-12). Many of us don't see the reason why we should embrace a change process. There is continuous resistance in our heart to new ideas, because we are still under the control and bondage of our wilderness condition (Galatians 4:3). This is what I refer to as the "Egyptization" effect. Our long stay in the world, which is Egypt, is affecting our relationship with God. As a result, we don't see the need for an improvement in the lives we live. Any sensible person should believe that there are better ways of doing the things they do. Going through Galatians 4:2, we would see that every child of God needs to go through an indoctrination process until, in the fullness of time, we start benefiting from the blessings in God's Kingdom. This is where creativity comes in. For instance, nothing stops a married woman from inventing a new recipe for the soup she cooks. We should try newness, in all we do. There used to be black and white cathode ray tube television, and today we have LED flat screen TVs. This is improvement. Cars are being designed with better aerodynamic streamlined features, and aesthetic beauty.

2. Repentance

A clean heart houses a steadfast spirit – the creative spirit within (Psalm 51:5). Repentance has a lot to do with reformation. This process is what Christ explained to Nicodemus as "Born Again." Repentance cannot be practised;

it has to come through the Holy Spirit, who will confront the devil's spirit living in us. This is when we will begin to show remorse for all our evil deeds.

3. Renewing our Minds

We must learn to think positive, all the time. Positive thinking gives rise to positive living. Romans 12:2 talks about the renewal of the mind: *And do not be conformed to this world, but be transformed by the renewing of your mind, that you may prove what is that good and acceptable and perfect will of God.*

The first thing to do once we have accepted Christ is to ensure that we do not carry over yesterday. We should see the reason behind God sending Jesus to redeem us. The Bible says in John 3:16 that He so loved the world.

4. Putting on the light of success

Dreaming about success is not enough. Jesus says that we must light it up, bring it out for all to see, and we must power it to the extent that it will "so shine" (Mathew 5:15-16). He painted this in the parable of the ten virgins also. Those who had enough oil in their lamps were the ones who valued longevity, because they had enough to burn till the bridegroom came. To those virgins, their ability to wait until the arrival of the groom and be with him is the success they were expecting, but they had to light up their perseverance till he came. Lighting the light of success has a lot to do with how creative we are. Do you fade out of relevance as easily as did the five virgins without oil in their lamps?

5. Ensure your creativity gives God glory

This is where many of us miss out. We have technologies today which are turning people's hearts away from God. Our work must give glory to God. We didn't create ourselves, He did, and accordingly we must be ready to give Him all the glory, not only from our mouths but through our actions and behaviour. If the results of our creative ideas can give Glory to God, we are on our way to success.

6. Be ready to learn – be more ready to listen

Learning is a process, and every process requires a step-by-step indoctrination, through knowledge acquisition, into an order of both physical and spiritual allies, with a view to becoming adaptable to the ideals of the order of an existing Heavenly authority. Every believer needs the authority to function as a son of God. And, as such we have to learn about Christ (Matthew 11:29). I have found out that:

To Learn is to Submit. To Submit is to Agree. To Agree is to Adopt. To Adopt is to Apply. And To Apply is to Adapt.

When we begin to apply what we have learned, we will begin to bear fruits that will abide (John 15:16). These fruits are the products of our creative intelligence. And we will begin to solve the problems in our lives and in the allies which we had subscribed to.

7. Be ready to accept constructive corrections

This is closely related to what we just explained above. Constructive corrections are products of effective research, and experiential, inborn wisdom. Wisdom is a product of knowledge and understanding. Those who accept creative corrections are seeing what they do as a service rendered to improve other people's lives. Selfish people are never creative. Proud people end up being consumers only. Non-creative people are, in most cases, low-class labourers who only carry out routine jobs, and have difficulty improving on what they do. They hardly accept new ideas. They are, also, in most cases, too methodical to bear fruit. They include those pastors who would not wait on the Holy Spirit to give them unction when they are preaching on the pulpit but would rather rely on what they have learned by rote. They practise speaking in tongues. They are like the Pharisees and Sadducees, who were never ready to accept the teachings of Christ.

8. Look ahead of today

We can only think about the events in recent days when we look to the future. Those who see ahead of today are those to whom God gives visions. The Bible says that the light of the body is the eyes (Matthew 6:22). This refers to the spiritual eyes. This process starts with our ability to find solutions to the common problems we see around us. If we can always think of how to make things better for the future, we will excel in creative thinking. This is why the parable of the ten virgins, in Matthew 25, is very important in our lives. Every day we are alive, we should make a determined effort to think ahead of today. Plan your life, or the devil will plan it for you. Look five years ahead of you. If you plan your life you will know where you need help, spiritually and physically. Sit down and describe yourself carefully on a piece of paper. Hand it over to someone to confirm that your description is accurate. Then ask yourself if the person you just described on that piece of paper will succeed in life with the qualities you listed. Also ask yourself if the person will reach Heaven.

Now that we know the process of creative intelligence, let us put our creativity to work.

CREATIVE PRAYERS

Until Jesus taught the disciples how to pray, the Angels could not do it. Not even Moses knew how to pray, because if he had, that pattern would have also been handed down to the Israelites, and there would have been no need for a retraining on how to revere God in prayers. Prior to the teaching in the Lord's Prayer, all that the Jews knew was how to demand from God and to sacrifice for their sins. A time came when there was not even food in the storehouse of the tabernacle (Malachi 3:8-10). As many of us still do today, they were denying God their resources. God never told Abel to make a sweet-tasting offering to Him. Noah also gave without God demanding it. Yet today we want God to talk to us before we can give for His work. Many of us have enjoyed free journals, and even Bibles, sponsored by others. We should let our consciences speak, if we are doing what is right. If our thinking is only about caring for ourselves, then we are not yet the Man God Made. This may be the reason why many are yet to experience peace in their spirit. Giving and prayers go hand in hand.

A story had it that one day a woman returned from her journey and asked her maid if she had being sleeping with her husband, referring to the stories she had heard of other women's experiences. And the maid, who was poor in English, said yes. The woman beat the hell out of her and sent her out of the house. When her husband came in that evening, there was a raging quarrel, until he called in their pastor. When they brought in the maid, they realised that what she had meant by sleeping with the husband was that she had never left the house all night but had slept at home after doing her chores.

Many of us may have had this encounter in our prayers to God because of our pronunciation. Some would pray God "press me" in the place of "bless me". Some will say "Lord ingrease me" instead of "increase me". Some will pray God for "bees" instead of "peace". In all, God knows your heart. Go ahead and pray for what you want, provided your heart is filled with that desire of yours. God values heartfelt prayers more than prayers that are said without conviction.

Let your heart feel the pulse of your needs. This is the only way it will take root in the spirit. The way many of us pray sometime seems to me as though we are having a quarrel with God. I am not surprised if some actually mean "warship" when they say that they "worship" God. We should not shoot at God with our prayers as if they are bullets or grenades. Your prayers should be filled with respect, adoration and honour unto God.

The following steps will lead us into praying creatively rather than just mumbling words that will seem as though we are abusing God. The book of Job 6:24-25 says: *Teach me, and I will hold my tongue: and cause me to understand wherein I have erred. How forcible are right words! but what doth your arguing reprove?*

When God teaches us and gives us the right words to pray with, our prayers will become forceful, putting things right in our lives. This is because there is no injustice in God's tongue (Job 6:30), which is the one that proceeds from the father, The Holy Spirit. The utterance of the Holy Spirit of God is the tongue of God. This is why praying in the spirit and speaking in tongues are evidence of one speaking from the throne of God. God answers only righteous prayers, and the Holy Spirit is righteous. If we pray by the Holy Spirit, our prayers will smell sweet savour unto God. And before we start praying, we should learn to exalt Him from our hearts with our voices. King David teaches us how to exalt God in our prayers in 1 Chronicles 29:11-13:

Thine, O LORD is the greatness, and the power, and the glory, and the victory, and the majesty: for all that is in the Heaven and in the Earth is thine; thine is the kingdom, O LORD, and thou art exalted as head above all. Both riches and honour come of thee, and thou reignest over all; and in thine hand is power and might; and in thine hand it is to make great, and to give strength unto all. Now therefore, our God, we thank thee, and praise thy glorious name.

From these verses we will be discussing the following as prerequisites that we must appreciate before we can start to pray:

1. You must be a child of God - Matthew 22:14.

2. You must continually seek repentance – 1 Chronicles 7:14

3. Humble yourself before God – Ecclesiastes 5:1

4. Know why you must pray – Matthew 19:26

5. Go into your closet, and not where people will admire what you are doing – Matthew 6:6

6. Convince yourself that God is in Heaven – Daniel 11:32

7. Ask God to strengthen you to win souls – Matthew 9:38

8. Love your neighbour as you love yourself, which is born out of you showing unbelievers the way to God-Matthew 12:31

9. Ask for daily bread. Let God know that you depend on His provision every day-Matthew 6:11

10. Ask for forgiveness, after forgiven yourself and those who offended you-Matthew 18:15-20, Matthew 6:12

11. Believe that you have received- this is where the power of creative imagination lies – Mark 11:24

The word of the Lord says: "Whatsoever we bind on Earth shall be bound in Heaven" (Matthew 18:18). Ask yourself what you want to keep bound forever, and why you were not getting results in your earlier attempt to keep the situation bound forever. Are you with the key of the Kingdom of Heaven (Matthew 16:19)? *And again Jesus says: "If two of you agree concerning anything on Earth, it shall be done for you by God in Heaven"* - Matthew 18:19. Who is agreeing with you? What is his/her attitude towards what you are praying for? These are questions we need to ask before we pray.

Some will wake up and start speaking tongues they cannot interpret. Many at times will also see people praying out of emotion, and as such they will begin to speak volumes of irrational words. A study of the Bible will reveal that before we can pray, there is something we should have done as explained below:

1. **Founding favour in the sight of God**

   This is borne out of your walk with God. King David once told God to search his heart to see if there was any iniquity in him. God has also challenged us to testify against him (Micah 6:3).

2. **The willingness of God to heal your situation**

   Job found favour in the sight of God, but the trial he was going through was a test of his faith, and as such God was not willing to intercept that process until the appointed time, when the devil must have satisfied himself.

3. **Faith in our prayer**

   Our faith speaks volumes. If we lack faith, there is no way we can pray God's word into action. We all know that God is Love and we can convince ourselves with the acts of Jesus, found in the gospels, which were the only evidence the disciples had seen that gave them the assurance that if they obeyed Christ greater things would manifest in their lives, and they succeeded. The Bible says "God so loved the World", including you and me. And we have learned time without number that His love is the reason behind all the testimonies of healing and favour from God. This is how faith works. With this assurance, we are supposed to dedicate our entire lives to the work of God, waiting for

Him to reward us (Hebrews 11:6). The problem with many of us is that we don't want to make sacrifices to do God's work (Psalms 50:5), yet we expect His reward. God is not a man and does not lie. He says in John 14:15-16 that those who do His command shall be rewarded with power from above. And with this power, the Holy Spirit will lead us through the path of righteousness, which will henceforth bring God's favour to us.

4. **Your sacrifice**

Sacrifice is a sign of fellowship with God. The sacrifice we make by being committed in our workplace because of our monthly salary is less than what God is expecting from us. This was the reason the disciples had to abandon their careers. When you sacrifice for the work of God, to do His command, Jesus will continuously advocate on your behalf, and as such you don't need long prayers because the Holy Spirit will take over from you the moment you are set to pray. We can see this in John 17, when Jesus had to pray for His disciples. Even in your weakness the church is praying for you, as in the case of Peter. Do not be a "one-man riot squad." Work in fellowship, and dedicate your time and resources. Make sure you attend all weekly church activities. People have built the church you see around today, which is the reason someone came to ensure that you were saved. What have you done to help the work of God?

We need to gather together more often than just on Sundays. If everyone behaved the way many of us do, we would be decimated by those who oppose Christianity. You cannot claim to be for God when you can comfortably stay at home while weekly activities are going on in your local church. Go, and hew your own dried firewood so as to keep our salvation jamboree fire burning.

CREATIVE WORSHIP (SINGING)

Many of us claim that we worship God in our songs, yet we do not know Him. Jesus told the Samaritan woman this at the well, when He said that the Samaritans worship the God they know nothing about (John 4:22). Creative singing helps the singer to see Heaven, and to see how God and His Angels are responding to the encomiums in the lyrics. After successfully going through the steps of a creative prayer, as shown above, the steps below will help us to sing creatively:

1. Understanding what the song is all about – is it a praise song or a worship song? A praise song is more of a victory song, while a worship song is more about surrendering our lives to God. Songs must have a prophetic undertone. They must be filled with the thoughts and the imagination of one speaking from the throne of God.

2. Timing is key – morning songs should be songs of

adoration, honour, praise, prophecy and vow. In the afternoon, it should be a song filled with lyrics of thanksgiving. And in the evening, it should be songs of praise and thanksgiving. In the night, before we sleep, our songs should be filled with dedication, dependence on His protection, promises of obedience and willingness to do God's will.

3. Who is singing the song matters – For the church praise and worship session, the song leader's heart must be filled with the spirit of God, he must be one with the heart of repentance. This will enable the leader to be focused and see Heaven all through the praise/worship session.

4. The environment where the song is being rendered to God matters too. Many would claim to be gospel artists when their hearts are actually not with God, and as such the reason behind the songs are defeated. The church gathering is another environment which can affect the purpose of the songs. Do the congregation know what they are doing? Can they visualize God in their hearts? This is another reason why we need to continually get them trained on what to do before coming into God's presence, and while they are in His presence. Moses told the congregation how they must appear before they could see God while they were in the wilderness. After that

experience they begged him not to make them see God again. In other words, they weren't ready to consecrate themselves to be acceptable to God. We must create an environment that is holy unto God – from our hearts to our worship arenas.

CREATIVE ASSOCIATION

Every gathering or association is only possible under the right sets of rules and regulations. In Exodus 23:20, God made it clear to us that some associations can brew evil. The question now is which association do we belong to – for evil or for good? The book of Amos 3:3 explains the underlying factor that can aid the association of people - They must agree and walk together! Creative association is the unification of people with a common objective aimed towards adding value to the lives of people in a society.

The act of "value-addition" is the act of godliness. For instance, the value addition proposed in Genesis 11:3-7, where men tried to build a tower that would reach Heaven to bring glory to themselves, is against the will of God for humans to fill the Earth, and this therefore, is an uncreative association.

We are told to abstain from all appearance of evil (1 Thessalonians 5:22). What does this mean? Is it that some things appear to be evil in nature? Is it that God created evil for us to see? We may be asking ourselves these questions. The truth is that the devil has manipulated the hearts of men to erect evil signposts and billboards wherever the head turns. Before we associate with people, we should be able to convince ourselves that we will not, as a result, go to hell.

Playing a Ludo game, for instance, is not evil. It is only evil when it involves the bet of money. Then it becomes a gambling instrument. At times, the playing of games takes people far away from God. We can steer our ship of association in the right direction when we know where to belong:

• Should Christians go to the club or see movies?

• Is it right for Christian men to have shampooed hair?

• Should Christian ladies wear mini-skirts and bodyhuggers?

• Should a Christian go to a party where alcohol is served?

• Should a Christian operate a brothel?

The answers to these questions lie in our conscience.

CREATIVE FELLOWSHIP

For what reasons have we gathered together? Do we really want to revere God? A creative fellowship is a fellowship that has God at the centre of its agenda, with a view towards supporting the vision of the church. Every church has a focus, to lead a set of people to God. Are we supporting the purpose of the calling upon the Man of God in our midst or we are comparing His ministry with where we are coming from? There is a reason for the new wine being stored in a new wine skin.

The book of 1 John 1:7 says: *But if we are living in the light of God's presence, just as Christ does, then we have wonderful fellowship and joy with one another, and the blood of Jesus His Son cleanses us from every sin.*

Jesus' prayer in John 17:21-22 is the heart of creative fellowship: *My prayer for all of them is that they will be of one heart and mind, just as you and I are, Father – that just as you are in me and I am in you, so they will be in us, and the world will believe you sent me. I have given them the glory you have given me – the glorious unity of being one - I in them and you in me, all being perfected into one – so that the world will know that you sent me and understands that you love them as much as you love me.*

The following actions are ingredients of a creative fellowship – a fellowship that will provide the solution to the problems in the church.

- Love one another (Romans 12:10, 13:8, John 15:12).
- Have the same mind towards one another (Romans 12:16).
- Confess your sins to one another (James 5:16).
- Forgive one another (Colossians 3:13; Ephesians 4:31-32; Matthew 18:21-35).
- Show hospitality to one another (Romans 15:17).
- Admonish one another (Hebrews 3:13; 10:25).
- Pray for one another (James 5:16).

- Bear one another's burdens (Galatians 6:2).

- Consider one another (Hebrews 10:24).

- Greet one another with a Holy kiss (Romans 16:16, 1 Peter 5:14, 2 Corinthians 13:12).

- Comfort one another (1 Thessalonians 4:18; 5:11).

- Edify one another (Romans 14:19).

- Teach one another (Colossians 3:16).

- Judge not one another (Romans 14:13).

- Serve one another (Galatians 5:13; John 13:1-17).

- Accept one another (Romans 15:7).

CREATIVE DESIRE

Desires are closely related to prayers. There is a verse of the Bible that seems to summarise what our desires before God should be. Philippians 4:8 says: *Finally, brethren, whatsoever things are true, whatsoever things are honest, whatsoever things are just, whatsoever things are pure, whatsoever things are lovely, whatsoever things are of good report; if there be any virtue, and if there be any praise, think on these things.*

This verse summarises the reasons why we actually would want God to bless us. Taking a look at each of these elements, we would see that the only desire that meets all these is the quest to do the work of God, and the gift that will enable us do that is the Holy Spirit of God. In John 7:37-39 Jesus also explains what we should desire most in our lives.

In the last day, that great day of the feast, Jesus stood and cried, saying, If any man thirst, let him come unto me, and drink. He that believeth on me, as the scripture hath said, out of his belly shall flow rivers of living water. (But this spake he of the Spirit, which they that believe on him should receive: for the Holy Ghost was not yet given; because that Jesus was not yet glorified.)

We can achieve this if we have a renewed mind, which only thinks of the price we would pay if we lose Heaven. Our desire is what drives our determination. Creative desire is therefore a desire that focuses on Christ, who is the wisdom of God. Once we have this divine wisdom we will stand firm in our drive to affect lives positively, because this is the whole essence of creativity. Adding value to lives is the arm of longevity. This is why we keep on praying that God should add value to our lives. This is the arm of God, which we all know is not too short to redeem anyone.

Let's look at some of the use of the word "desire" in the Bible and what is meant.

Jeremiah 31:32 says that God is a husband to the church. And John 3:29 depicts Jesus as the bridegroom. We can therefore borrow the words in Genesis 3:16 *...thy desire shall be to thy Husband, and He shall rule over thee*, to mean that our desire as the bride of Jesus is to love Jesus and whatsoever He commands. Psalms 73:25 says: *Whom have I in Heaven but thee? and there is none upon Earth that I desire beside thee.*

In the beginning God ordained that the Man God Made should tend His garden. That garden today is the church of Christ, which bears witness of His blood spilled at Golgotha. Our desires have the powers to drive us into numerous worldly wants. Many times, what we desire may take our attention from God and His church, because we tend to become selfish as we provide food, shelter, and clothing for ourselves.

We may end up spending money travelling for fun, and if possible we would want to see all the wonderful cities of the world at the expense of the work of God. Then a time comes when conscience starts to prick us, making us to know that we had gone astray, and some of us would try to make a U-turn to make things right. This is what God meant in Genesis 6:5: *And God saw that the wickedness of man was great in the Earth, and that every imagination of the thoughts of his heart was only evil continually.*

Why is God so concerned? Ephesians 5:23 says why: *For the husband is the head of the wife, even as Christ is the head of the church: and He is the saviour of the body.*

Have we allowed Christ to take over our desires too? Throughout Scripture our desires have been seen by God as evil and wicked from the days of our youth (Jeremiah 17:9). There is the belief in us that once we become Christians, our desires are in tune with God's purpose provided we can support this with some verses in the Bible. There are shortcomings to this claim. In most cases it is not far from what is said in Romans 7:19: *For the good that I would I do not: but the evil which I would not, that I do.*

Many times too, we are also pushed into working against the purpose of Christ, which is soul winning, all in the name of self-righteousness, and the popular Biblical declaration that tells us not to allow a witch to live (Exodus 22:18). In our prayers, our attitude towards our neighbours when we pray for their downfall is often born out of the fact that our desire is to live without opposition. The Disciples of Jesus, James and John, felt this way too when they met opposition while with Jesus: *And when his disciples James and John saw this, they said, Lord, wilt thou that we command fire to come down from Heaven, and consume them, even as Elias did? But he turned, and rebuked them, and said, Ye know not what manner of spirit ye are of. For the Son of man is not come to destroy men's lives, but to save them. - Luke 9:54-56*

Let us go through the following verses, which will explain what kinds of desires we often bear in our hearts. These desires are not creative; rather, they are uncreative and destructive. *Luke 22:24: And there was also a strife among them, which of them should be accounted the greatest.*

Mark 10:37: They said unto him, Grant unto us that we may sit, one on thy right hand, and the other on thy left hand, in thy glory.

James 4:2,3: Ye lust, and have not: ye kill, and desire to have, and cannot obtain: ye fight and war, yet ye have not, because ye ask not. Ye ask, and receive not, because ye ask amiss, that ye may consume it upon your lusts.

The following also explains what creative desires are:
John 5:30: I can of mine own self do nothing: as I hear, I judge: and my judgment is just; because I seek not mine own will, but the will of the Father which hath sent me.
John 6:38: For I came down from Heaven, not to do mine own will, but the will of Him that sent me.

The question we should be asking ourselves now is: How much of our prayers and intercessions, asking, knocking, seeking, waiting and hoping, is done with a view towards getting God to do what He want us to do? Our desire should be to do the will of God, here on Earth.

CREATIVE PREACHING

Another name for the act of preaching is "homiletic". Jesus' message was straight to the point: "repent, for the Kingdom of God, which you had desired for ages, is now living with you." Preaching is all about providing a one-off Godly answer to the problems in the society. If this is achieved, then the people will see the handiwork of God in their lives through practical living.

A creative preacher must think of how he/she could reach the congregation with bits of information, like laying bricks to bring into existence the erection of a Godly thought in the hearts of the children of God. This shows that the preacher must be creative and have a sound mind and a sound doctrine of the Christian faith (2 Timothy 2:15).

The creative preacher, since he/she is more concerned about value addition, would usually ask the question: what is most needed now? How can I lead them to Christ in the most fascinating way? This is because every message or sermon points to one fact: making everyone of us become the Man God Made, so that we can do the will of God, and thereafter merit Heaven at the end of the day.

We would be learning from Jesus in the book of Matthew 11:25-30:

At that time Jesus answered and said, I thank thee, O Father, Lord of Heaven and Earth, because thou hast hid these things from the wise and prudent, and hast revealed them unto babes. Even so, Father: for so it seemed good in thy sight. All things are delivered unto me of my Father: and no man knoweth the Son, but the Father; neither knoweth any man the Father, save the Son, and he to whomsoever the Son will reveal Him. Come unto me, all ye that labour and are heavy laden, and I will give you rest. Take my yoke upon you, and learn of me; for I am meek and lowly in heart: and ye shall find rest unto your souls. For my yoke is easy, and my burden is light.

The knowledge of God does not necessarily dwell with titles: Archbishop, Bishop, Most Reverend, Right Reverend,

General Superintendent, etc. It resides with those who are willing to learn of Jesus – "babes." The only way we can take His yoke upon us is when we can have the same character as Jesus: meek and lowly.

We can learn the following facts from what we just read above:

1. Jesus thanked God in the presence of everybody – confessing Him before them, and as such pointing everyone's attention towards Heaven.

2. He also made everyone there present know that God is the only one who can reveal the solutions to their problems, which are hidden in mysteries that even the devil cannot comprehend.

3. He made all present also know that He only does what God approves. This will definitely make everyone know that the answer to their ill situation lies in God's hands, and as such they must wait on God's approval.

4. He confirmed that He sees God. This would give those present the assurance of God's intervention in their cases. The pure in heart will certainly see God (Matthew 5:7). A preacher who does not see God has no right to preach. A church music leader who does not see God should not handle praise and worship. A prayer leader who does not see God should not lead prayers, and so on.
   How can we see God? Jesus has shown Him to us

(Matthew 11:27, John 14:7-11). God approves Jesus throughout His life on Earth. Has God approved you? God can only approve those who are in Christ: *And to be in Christ, we must study the word of God (John 15:3, John 17:17, 2 Timothy 2:15).*

5. He knew those who needed the salvation: they labour in pain and they are heavy laden. A sermon that is gotten out of the preacher's personal needs of donations and offerings will only lead people into hell. Christ's sermons were geared towards salvation, and what those He ministered to needed to do to obtain everlasting life. Everlasting life is the beauty of salvation and it is in two phases – here on Earth, fulfilling your days, and in Heaven – everlasting life. Those who have obtained everlasting life, whose names have been written in the book of life, live a memory of godliness behind in the hearts of people when they die. This is one easy and quick way to know if those who are dead around us will make Heaven. A creative preacher must put a round peg in a round hole. Our church is founded on the principle of salvation – leading God's children to Heaven, through the teaching of the wisdom that will enable them execute the will of God here on Earth. This is captured in our church's mission statement: To Recruit, Train, and Spiritually Empower men, women, youths and children with the wisdom to execute the will of God on Earth.

6. He gave them a glimpse of the solution they need – Rest! And the, rest they need will come from no other person but Himself. Jesus revealed to them over and over again that there is no other path to salvation but Himself. What do we see today? People are being cajoled into believing in all manner of demons as a means to having peace.

7. He showed them the process that will lead to that peace – "Take my yoke upon you, and learn of me; for I am meek and lowly in heart: and ye shall find rest unto your souls." Further in verse 30 He gave them an opportunity to imagine what He meant by what He just said.

Any sermon preached with the above concept in mind is a creative sermon, and it will definitely touch lives, better than a mere collocation of words and phonetic rendering of words, acquired through long fruitless nights spent in the acquisition of dictionary vocabularies.

CREATIVE MARRIAGE

I woke up from a nap on the evening of the 25th of November 2011 at about 7 pm with this definition of marriage resounding in my spirit:

Marriage is an erotic, passionate and inseparable spiritual bond existing between two unique persons of opposite sex, male and female, with a common destiny to fulfil, who had lived separate lives supposedly aimed at equipping them with the skills and wisdom that should enable them to execute the will of God on Earth, which is the common destiny they share.

This definition negates the "contractual" term often used in the common definitions of marriage seen in the English dictionaries. In the first day of the marriage, the union is said to be "consumed" in an event called "marriage consummation." This fulfils the very first line qualifier, "erotic, passionate."

Why do we get married? Some will say it is so that we do not fornicate, while others will say they just want a companion. I have also heard men say they need a working woman who will help them with money in order to make ends meet. Many of course have got married because they were told to marry, as age was no longer on their side. Some women would say they wanted someone who was rich to help them and their families out.

A creative marriage is a marriage that seeks to please God, because God is the origin of any marriage between a man and a woman. So none of the above reasons truly answer the question, "why should we marry?" We should go to the author of marriage Himself to lead us to the truth about marriage.

And the Lord God said, It is not good that the man should be alone; I will make him an help meet for him. - Genesis 2:18.

Therefore shall a man leave his father and his mother, and shall cleave unto his wife: and they shall be one flesh. - Genesis 2:24

From these two verses we see that a creative marriage is a marriage that is founded on God's creative intelligence in all ramifications of life. Here is the conclusion of Genesis 2:18 and 24:

1. A creative marriage is a marriage in which the male and the female exist as one flesh. The term "flesh" includes our reasoning abilities. It has to do with how we make our decisions, and how we see the future.

2. At no time must either the male or the female in this union exist independently. This includes sexual intimacy and decision-making. The man must wait for his wife to agree before he can take any action. The same applies to the wife. It is not a good thing for man to exist independently of his wife. This is what those who follow occult beliefs miss. Once they can exist in thoughts, decisions and emotions, independently, the marriage union is already broken. If they cannot trust each other, there is no marriage and both of them would start to live in deceit. This is where the devil comes in, because he is the father of deceit and a master of it (John 8:44).

3. We all need help in one way or the other. The woman is a man's helpmeet. In other words, she is the only one who can meet the help of the man. I would advise that before any man seeks advice from outside, he first needs to consult his wife. If your wife is always indecisive when you bring a

matter to her, you may have married a woman who was meant for another man. This may be hard to believe. If you know both of you are incompatible, then teach each other what needs to be changed.

4. The next thing we see, in verse 24, is the word "cleave." The intransitive form of the word is defined by Merriam-Webster's dictionary as "to adhere firmly and closely or loyally and unwaveringly". So a creative marriage is a marriage that finds a way of ensuring that the man and the woman adhere firmly to each other. They must be close in everything, including discussion. They must be loyal to each other, obeying themselves in line with godly principles, and the union must not waver even if there is no food to eat, no clothing to wear, no money for school fees, etc. A woman should never drive her husband crazy because they need money, and a man who would want to put pressure on his wife all in the name of looking for money should desist, because it is ungodly.

CREATIVE EMPLOYMENT

I have decided to add this also, though it may look absurd here. Many people are unable to take the work of God seriously because of the kind of job they do. Some of us tell lies to remain faithful to the company's overall goal and objective. A creative job is a job that gives you the opportunity to say no to unethical practices, so as to remain in good standing with God. This is because creativity is about adding value to lives; our cheating, lying, aggressive habits will only make people sad as we work with them. Do not let your job take you to hell.

You can now add your own creative ideas, geared towards adding value to lives wherever you live. Everything done creatively receives the approval of God. The devil is not creative, because he never created anything. The devil's main purpose is to deface what God has created. This is the meaning of the devil moving to and fro and looking for whom to devour (1 Peter 5:8).

Think, watch, pray, meditate and create something which will add value to your life. It is our responsibility to make this world better before we die. Isaiah 42:22 speaks of God's ultimate concern for the world he created: No one says restore. Restore every situation you come across to its intended original form. Shalom!

CHAPTER ELEVEN

MAN MADE FOR LOVE

For Adam to have named all manner of beast in the field shows that the Man God Made was made for love, hence no man can function successfully in an environment that grows thorns of hatred. For Adam not to have chased the serpent away also shows that he was a man filled with the spirit of hospitality. God strolling into the garden also demonstrates the fact that He had been enjoying the receptive fellowship he was having with Adam. Since God is love, it would be right to say that Adam existed in love, hence love always visited him. What then is love?

Beloved, let us love one another: for love is of God; and every one that loveth is born of God, and knoweth God. He that loveth not knoweth not God; for God is love. In this was manifested the love of God toward us, because that God sent his only begotten Son into the world, that we might live through him. Herein is love, not that we loved God, but that he loved us, and sent his Son to be the propitiation for our sins. Beloved, if God so loved us, we ought also to love one another. No man hath seen God at any time.

If we love one another, God dwelleth in us, and his love is perfected in us. Hereby know we that we dwell in him, and he in us, because he hath given us of his Spirit – 1 John 4:7-13.

Humility is an attribute that helps us to love one another. If Adam had not been humble he would not have attracted the presence of God, which was the only reason why he could name all that he named before his fall. We can shine if we are truly humble and not carried away by pride.

I once watched a movie titled *Two Days in Paris*, the story of Marion, a French-born photographer living in New York City with Jack, her boyfriend, who was a neurotic, hypochondriacal, chain-smoking, heavily tattooed interior designer. They tried to mend their sinful, unromantic love affair by taking a trip to Venice to reignite the passion in their relationship. Marion later learned that Jack had numerous ex-lovers whom he still dated. She became increasingly uncomfortable because of the language barrier between her and Jack and the pain of his neglect. Marion was fighting within herself to manage her insecurities about love, their relationship and her continuous spontaneous outbursts of anger.

I learned from the movie how difficult it is to rekindle a decaying unholy love relationship. Whenever we do things without God's approval we end up harbouring the burning effects of sins within us, and this will to a large extent deny us peace. What happened in that story was a mixture of sinful cohabitation between a man and a woman, drug addiction, lack of spiritual knowledge, infatuation and lack of proper upbringing. We can summarise all that to mean the absence of God in their lives. There is no love elsewhere except in Christ Jesus.

Until we confess our sins and become united with Christ in our thoughts and actions, there is no way we can experience love. Love has to do with self denial. Love is possible where there is unity. This is the reason why God is love, because God the Father, God the Son and God the Holy Spirit are united in purpose and action.

In the book of John 5:19, Jesus gave them this answer: *"I tell you the truth, the Son can do nothing by himself; he can do only what he sees his Father doing, because whatever the Father does the Son also does. (NIV)*

There is a love-web in Heaven. At the baptism of Jesus, God the Father spoke in Heaven as the Holy Spirit descended on Jesus, the Son. We can say here that what linked Jesus to God while He was here on Earth is the Holy Spirit. Jesus is now in Heaven with God the Father, and the Holy Spirit is given to us here on Earth to create a perfect bond that will link us to God. We said earlier that God is love (1 John 4:8). This means that once we are linked to Heaven through the Holy Spirit, we become connected to the spring of love-the love-web of God. When more people are connected to God this way, all of us who exist in this bond will begin to love God, do God's command, and love one another.

Mark 12:30-31: *Love the Lord your God with all your heart and with all your soul and with all your mind and with all your strength. The second is this: Love your neighbour as yourself.* There is no commandment greater than these.

From the foregoing, we can see the love-web in Heaven with God and Jesus in the centre, sitting at the right hand of the father and connected to all faithful disciples through the Holy Spirit. Our link to God through the Holy Spirit is like a two-headed arrow, showing that we must agree with God in our thoughts.

Based on this, it is necessary for us to know what we need to do to achieve this interrelationship with God and his disciples.

The love-web first tells us that the Holy Spirit is given to disciples, and not to those who merely claim to be born again. It is given to those who are willing to do the work of God (Acts 1:8), and by so doing, they will experience the manifestation of God's love. This implies that the reason we have malice and hatred in the church is because many of us are yet to grow to disciple status. Once this happens, love will dynamically flow between the disciples. The disciples are those Christ referred to in His prayer in John 17:20-25:

My prayer is not for them alone. I pray also for those who will believe in me through their message, that all of them may be one,

Father, just as you are in me and I am in you. May they also be in us so that the world may believe that you have sent me. I have given them the glory that you gave me, that they may be one as we are one: I in them and you in me. May they be brought to complete unity to let the world know that you sent me and have loved them even as you have loved me. Father, I want those you have given me to be with me where I am, and to see my glory, the glory you have given me because you loved me before the creation of the world. Righteous Father, though the world does not know you, I know you, and they know that you have sent me. I have made you known to them, and will continue to make you known in order that the love you have for me may be in them and that I myself may be in them.

From this portion of the Bible, we can infer the following as the doings of someone living in the Love of God:

1. Receive the message of salvation.

2. Believe in Jesus Christ.

3. Increase in the wisdom of God.

4. Be a part of the Christian community.

5. Love one another through care – in prayers and fellowship. Avoid anger, quarrel, back biting, etc.

6. Ensure you are in Christ continually.

7. Live in the glory of God through your deeds of restoration, as you preach the gospel. Christ told Peter

that he should use his salvation to save others: Jesus Christ said to Peter, "When you are converted, strengthen the brethren," - Luke 22:32.

8. Obey every command of God through the Holy Spirit: be watchful, you will be hearing and seeing. Your dreams will come alive once you are in that bond. You will see yourself doing the work of rescue and deliverance in your dreams.

9. Make sure you do not forsake the gathering of God's children so as to build your faith in God.

10. Preach the gospel to others so that they can be likewise saved.

As we go through all these stages of activities, we become more focus on the work of God, and His love will flow down like running streams of living waters. The Holy Spirit will then take the centre stage of our thought process, and we will begin to see the need to consider how other people feel about our daily actions.

From the Bible, I came across the fact that those who have grown the ladder to discipleship are easily forgiven by God when they err, because they rarely do. What baffles me is why David ate the consecrated bread in the Altar of God with his soldiers and he went scot-free (1 Samuel 21:1-6, Mark 2:23-28). Again Moses sinned against God, yet God still allowed him to see the land of Canaan, though he never entered, but his dead body was defended by Angel Michael (Jude 1:9).

Aaron was in sin with Miriam when they spoke against Moses, but he never became a leper. Adam sinned and he was thrown out of his only known home – why? Abraham lied and he was not punished. Jacob deceived his father, which was a grievous offence and he went free without a curse, because Isaac later discovered the trick he had played on him. God even warned Laban not to say any word to Jacob, whether good or evil, Genesis 31:24.

The mercy of God is indeed difficult to predict. This was exactly the meaning of the parable of Jesus in Matthew 20:1-16, where Jesus says that those who started early and those who started late will be paid the same wages. What He referred to here is the everlasting love of God, not telling us that we can repent whenever we feel like it. If He had meant that we can repent whenever we feel it is convenient for us, He would not have told the disciples to dust their feet and lay a curse on whoever rejected the gospel (Luke 9:3-5). That parable is a complete picture of the availability of his eternal grace for us all, made available the very day He was crucified upon the Altar in Golgotha.

CHAPTER TWELVE

MAN MADE FOR SERVICE

The book of Nehemiah tells us what service is all about. Now that you are experiencing the love of God, you should know that you are created to serve. This is the only way to greatness.

The Man God Made was instructed to tend the Garden of God. This is the hallmark of service. In whatever we do, if God is not the focus, we will be like someone laying bricks for a house in the rains. The Earth as we know it today is made up of ourselves, our families, our societies and our faith (God).

As an engineer, I know that when the moving parts of a machine are not lubricated we may begin to hear creaking friction sounds, and this sound will make us uncomfortable. The parts may end up becoming worn out due to the action of wear and tear. The work of the lubricant is to ensure that as the parts work together in achieving the goal of production, they will serve throughout their useful lives. In the following list, we will be discussing what God made man for – the calling upon all of us, and the goal of that service.

SERVICE TO OURSELF

- Raising personal altars
- Fasting and prayers
- Studying the Bible
- Hearing the word of God and meditation
- Sacrifices to the works of God, especially soul winning
- Obedience to God
- Personal hygiene
- Balanced diet
- Physical exercise
- Sanitation
- Clothing/shelter
- Healthy habits
- Safety and security

SERVICE TO OUR FAMILY

- Raising a family altar
- Fasting and Prayers
- Studying the Bible
- Family Evangelism
- Family sacrifices towards the work of God
- Family hygiene
- Balanced diet
- Physical exercise
- Sanitation

- Clothing/shelter
- Healthy habits
- Safety and security

SERVICE TO OUR SOCIETY

- Raising a national altar
- Fasting and Prayers
- Honesty and integrity
- Law abiding, provided it does not contravene God's command
- Building schools
- Building low-cost housing
- Providing skill training to others
- Providing Employment etc

SERVICE TO OUR FAITH

- Support to build Church altars
- Fasting and Prayers
- Studying the Bible
- Welfare
- Church attendance
- Praise and worship
- Writing Christian books
- Defending your faith
- Soul winning

If we neglect any of these we will find it difficult to experience the peace of God in our lives. The question we should be asking ourselves now is: how have we fared in these dimensions of service as individuals? The Bible says (Proverbs 22:4): *By humility and the fear of the Lord are riches, and honour, and life.*

We all need riches, honour and life. This is what explains the Glory of God in our lives. When God lives in us, we will experience all that is said in Proverbs 22:4. We have spent years schooling; from the elementary classes to the tertiary institutions, simply because we need a paper qualification that certifies that we can serve either in industry, government establishments, schools etc. But we have also, in most cases, forgotten about the ultimate reason why God created man; which was to tend His garden. Which garden are you tending for God? Are you the type who sows tares in His garden? Even if we are prepared to serve now, are we ready to drop our worldly wisdom for the wisdom of God? In Matthew 11:29 Jesus says: *Take my yoke upon you, and learn of me; for I am meek and lowly in heart: and ye shall find rest unto your souls.*

This verse explains the fact that Jesus wants to ride on us as a horse owner would do, so that whenever He draws the yoke, we respond. This was what He showed us by riding on the ass into Jerusalem. If we don't learn about Christ, there is no way we can be like Him. The classification of these services that is required of us can be summed up to represent the full meaning of the word, LOVE. It is a requirement in Heaven that we must love – Mark 12:30-31: *And thou shalt love the Lord thy God with all thy heart, and with all thy soul, and with all thy mind, and with all thy strength: this is the first commandment. And the second is like, namely this, Thou shalt love thy neighbour as thyself. There is none other commandment greater than these. - Deuteronomy 6:5.* (See also, Leviticus 19:18, Matthew 5:43, Matthew 19:19, Matthew 22:39, Romans 13:9, Galatians 5:14, James 2:8.)

Our neighbours include our families, the congregation and the larger society. If we can truly love ourselves and our neighbours, we can be able to love God (1 John 4:20). From here, we will be discussing these services in turn:

SELF SERVICE
I have discovered that though many people claim to love themselves, they actually hate themselves. Many of us used to drink alcohol or smoke for instance. For those who engaged in all manner of atrocities just to provide food for themselves, can they claim to love themselves too? Many of the illnesses that bedevil us today are the results of the lives we lived in the past. To ensure that the effects of our past sins are watered down, many of us have run to the church, and when we do not get results we also run into the hands of all manner of

spiritualists. I read how Michael Jackson had to take deadly painkiller drugs daily to stay alive towards his last sorrowful days on Earth. Yet this was a young man with lots of talent which would have blessed the world. Rather than live uprightly before God, we have in most cases chosen the path summarised in the following Bible verses: *For from within, out of the heart of men, proceed evil thoughts, adulteries, fornications, murders, Thefts, covetousness, wickedness, deceit, lasciviousness, an evil eye, blasphemy, pride, foolishness: All these evil things come from within, and defile the man. - Mark 7:21-23*

If we can avoid all these, we can truly tell ourselves that we love ourselves. And no evil will befall us.

FAMILY SERVICE

Closely related to what we discussed above is how well we can claim to have served our families. This is where Adam and Eve failed. They missed God's plan, and they missed everything. Is the family altar burning with fire? Are we laying aside grudges for the sake of love and unity? Can we really say today that we are happy, living together as one in our homes? Forgiveness is measured in what I will call the "Tolerance Multiplier" (TM) – Seventy times seven (Matthew 18:22).

This is the starting point of our service to our families. The devil will never want a formidable family to last long. Every time, he will sow seeds of discord enshrined in worldly pleasures in our hearts so that we can disagree over little things. We all, therefore, must make sure we play our own part in ensuring that the family altar is alive with the fire of God. We must make a determined effort to get musical instruments into the home, preferably a keyboard so that we can have a spirit-filled worship service at home. I have heard many women attack their husbands over the provisions in the house using 1 Timothy 5:8 as a yardstick. "Infidel," as used in 1 Timothy 5:8, means one who does not have faith – that is, the ungodly. Provision is not only in food, shelter, clothing, cars etc, it includes spiritual provision: ensuring that we all live our lives in the plan of God. This is why we need to go out for family evangelism and welfare service to the needy. Our environments must be neat to show that we have God living in our hearts.

SERVICE OF SOCIETY

We can serve society by creating avenues through which they can become closer to God. This is the type of service rendered to the Jews by the Roman Centurion: *And a certain centurion's servant, who was dear unto him, was sick, and ready to die. And when he heard of Jesus, he sent unto him the elders of the Jews, beseeching him that he would come and heal his servant. And when they came to Jesus, they besought him instantly, saying, That he was worthy for whom he should do this: For he loveth our nation, and he hath built us a synagogue. - Luke 9:2-5*

From what the people said, it can be seen that the centurion was not a Jew, yet he rendered that service to honour God, to ensure that society served God. If an unbeliever could do this, what have we done as believers in raising national altars where we can serve God? We can become leaders in our societies and display the attributes of humility, honesty and integrity. We should also take it upon ourselves to fast and pray for our nation, crying to God against every injustice in our societies. We must be ready to join other Christians in obeying Christian holidays as days in which we must remain obedient to God and seek for His intervention in the politics of our nation, and also pray for the presence of righteous people in government. We must be law-abiding citizens, provided such law does not contravene the defence of your Faith. Many have developed the software we use today in our various walks of life. The Google search engine, for instance, has helped the work of God greatly. We also have many other scientific feats that are making the work of God less strenuous – airplanes, ships, automobiles, printing presses, satellites etc. What have you contributed to society?

SERVICE OF FAITH

As people who love God, it is our responsibility to build worship centres all over the place where we can render praise unto Him. Our contributions of tithes and offerings go a long way towards keeping us closer to God, because we are storing treasures for the work of God, and our hearts will be in God's work. We should teach and preach the word of God, and live by the word. This service supersedes every other service in our lives. We are commanded to love God with all our hearts, minds and souls. There is nothing that is more important than this.

The Bible tells us that the fear of the Lord is the beginning of wisdom (Proverbs 9:10). Do we fear God in everything we do? Do we really value our Faith? Are we those who behave like the Egyptians when we are in Egypt? Do we pay lip service to our love for God? We can make amends today and really love God, because He loved us first (1 John 4:19). We should not forsake God's gathering, Hebrews 10:25. While I was growing up, crusades were all over the place. Today, millions of dollars are spent on crusades that hardly change lives. We should render welfare services even to the unsaved as a means to woo them into our fold.

We must ask God to inspire us so that we can write Christian books that focus on salvation, and become musical artists so that we can release spirit-filled musical albums. We should also harness the media for God's work – internet, radio, TV, journals, handbills etc. You must not be a pastor until you can print a simple handbill that says "Jesus Loves You." It is high time we supported the work of the Gospel, if we haven't started yet. Some people translated the Bible into different languages so that we can read it today. What will God remember us for, as Nehemiah called God to remembrance in Nehemiah 13? Are we going the ways of the Pharisees and Scribes – the religious?

He answered and said unto them, Well hath Esaias prophesied of you hypocrites, as it is written, This people honoureth me with their lips, but their heart is far from me. Howbeit in vain do they worship me, teaching for doctrines the commandments of men. - Isaiah 29:13 Matthew 15:8-9

God is ever ready to rewards our labour in His vineyard - Mark 10:30, Hebrews 11:6

I will conclude this chapter with the advice the Angel spoke to me when I was contemplating on whether I should answer this call or not. And that advice is, "God is watching you, if you don't do it, no one will do it for you." It is time to act - tomorrow may be too late.

CHAPTER THIRTEEN

MAN MADE TO SUCCEED

Is your life successful? What then is success? Most people see it in terms of achieving their dreams: riches, fame, favour, prominence and power. To me, people who are successful enjoy spiritual security, financial security, emotional security/stability, being surrounded by many admirers and their ability to enjoy the fruits of their labour. They are seen as role models, and many would prefer to use them as their mentors.

King Solomon, in Ecclesiastes 6:1-2, wondered why some people whom God has blessed with riches were unable to enjoy them. He saw this as "vexation of spirit."

This is what many miss. Today many of us define success as the material achievements we have around us. The church does this too; the definition of its success is measured by the numbers of their members, building size, the pastor's fame and the money in their bank accounts.

God's definition of success is somewhat different. God measures our success by our obedience and faithfulness to Him. He judges how we have employed the talents and gifts of the Holy Spirit that He gave to us in making the world a better place where everyone can regard Him through our own efforts of evangelism.

Jesus couldn't have qualified as a successful person by worldly standards of materialism. He achieved redemption for us all, and that is just enough for God.

What then is success? Why are we failing? We can learn from Adam's fall. See what the Bible says:

All scripture is given by inspiration of God, and is profitable for doctrine, for reproof, for correction, for instruction in righteousness. That the man of God may be perfect, thoroughly furnished unto all good works. - 2 Timothy 3:16-17

From the context above, we can say that we are failing because we lack reproof, correction, and the instruction that will take us through the path of righteousness. We then become imperfect, unthorough and without good works.

Our good works show when we have the heart of God. Then we become admired by everybody. Once this happens, we are on our way to success. The most important instrument in this path of human development and enculturation is the word of God. This word is what builds faith in us. *Hebrews 11:1 says: Now Faith is being sure of what we hope for and certain of what we do not see. And true faith not only believes it but knows it and expects it will happen.*

How do we receive faith? *Romans 10:17 says: So then, faith comes by hearing, and hearing by the word of God.*

Jesus defines Faith, as ...has not seen yet believes, in John 20:29. This is how faith works. You have not seen what you are expecting, but you have a reason to hope for it because of the substance of faith that you see around you, for example, the testimonies of others. The above verse shows that the act of hearing is made possible by the word of God. It involves two stages:

1. Spiritual hearing made possible through understanding the knowledge of God.
2. The right judgement of every word of God through the help of the Holy Spirit.

For Eve to accept the devil's proposal shows that she had lost faith in God. If Adam also had faith in the word of God, He would have cautioned Eve not to go near that tree, not when God had revealed to them the spiritual reason behind that instruction – "they shall die." As many children would want to touch a hot kettle, so also many of us want to taste the bitterness sin offers before we say no to the devil.

The parable of the sower shows that the sower went on and on sowing, yet only 25% of that effort was rewarded. Many of us are quick to expect success, and when we are not seeing success we get discouraged.

God created the world, and only a portion of that world became light. Does that deter Him? No! He rather went

ahead and separated the light from the darkness. In that light
(advantage) He invested His creative time. This was why
Jesus asked them in Mark 4:13: *And he said unto them, Know
ye not this parable? and how then will ye know all parables?* This
to me literally explains Luke 21:19, where Jesus says: *in your
patience possess ye your souls.*

The key to success is patience coupled with tireless sowing.
This is why the Bible tells us that the only licence to reaping
in joy is sowing in tears – invest every second of your time
positively. Adam didn't sow in that garden – God had the
garden perfectly in place, hence he never valued the effect of
the sin he was about to commit. I feel that he didn't explore
the resources in that garden. He should have asked God how
the gold in the land of Havillah was to be mined and used,
for instance:

*And a river went out of Eden to water the garden; and from
thence it was parted, and became into four heads. The name of
the first is Pison: that is it which compasseth the whole land of
Havilah, where there is gold; And the gold of that land is good:
there is bdellium and the onyx stone.* - Genesis 2:11

What surprised me was that it had to be the grandsons of
Cain who finally became the first inventors (Genesis 4:19-
22). If we look into society, it seems as if the ungodly are the
ones finding solutions to the problems of productivity. Must
we rely on Egypt to succeed? Many so-called believers can stay

up all day and night praying without thinking. Jesus was thinking when they brought the woman "caught in the very act" to Him (John 8:8). We must watch before praying (Matthew 26:41). A thoughtful watch will lead to success, because we will know the exact prayer points to raise before God. Thinking is spiritual communication. During the process of thinking, our mind is connected to the immortal spatial realm of the spirits, which holds the secret to the future. And so, when we watch, we will know what obstacles to remove from our path to success.

We have not been succeeding as God intends because we seem to be too comfortable – maybe because we have people we can easily beg from. The Garden of Eden was a comfortable home; hence they lost it to their carelessness. Necessity is the mother of invention, they say. And in my early days in the science class, I was told that science is about discovery. This is the essence of the secret things in Deuteronomy 29:29. If we must succeed we must be ready to keep on hoping and sowing until we get our success back on track. For this to happen, this is the secret:

- We must seek and love Righteousness:

  But seek ye first the kingdom of God, and his righteousness; and all these things shall be added unto you. - Matthew 6:33

  Thou lovest righteousness, and hatest wickedness: therefore God, thy God, hath anointed thee with the oil of gladness above thy fellows. - Psalms 45:7, Hebrew 1:9

- We must seek after the wisdom of God:

  Blessed is the man that walketh not in the counsel of the ungodly, nor standeth in the way of sinners, nor sitteth in the seat of the scornful. But his delight is in the law of the Lord; and in his law doth he meditate day and night. And he shall be like a tree planted by the rivers of water, that bringeth forth his fruit in his season; his leaf also shall not wither; and whatsoever he doeth shall prosper. - Psalms 1:1-3

- We must trust in the Lord – the whole essence of faith:

  Trust in the Lord with all thine heart; and lean not unto thine own understanding. In all thy ways acknowledge him, and he shall direct thy paths. Be not wise in thine own eyes: fear the Lord, and depart from evil. It shall be health to thy navel, and marrow to thy bones. Honour the Lord with thy substance, and with the first fruits of all thine increase: So shall thy barns be filled with plenty, and thy presses shall burst out with new wine. - Proverbs 3:5-10

We are also told in the book of Nahum 1:7 that the Lord knows those who trust in Him.

- We must work to earn God's approval – Don't be one of those who are out to please pastors through appearing to serve and become the agents of the devil when the pastor is not there.

  And they shall build houses, and inhabit them; and they shall plant vineyards, and eat the fruit of them. They shall not build, and another inhabit; they shall not plant, and another eat: for as the days of a tree are the days of my people, and mine elect shall long enjoy the work of their hands. They shall not labour in vain, nor bring forth for trouble; for they are the seed of the blessed of the LORD, and their offspring with them. -Isaiah 65:21-23

The Spirit itself beareth witness with our spirit, that we are the children of God: And if children, then heirs; heirs of God, and joint-heirs with Christ; if so be that we suffer with him, that we may be also glorified together. For I reckon that the sufferings of this present time are not worthy to be compared with the glory which shall be revealed in us. - Romans 8:16-18

- We must be firm in our spirit that God can provide for you:

  He that spared not his own Son, but delivered him up for us all, how shall he not with him also freely give us all things? - Romans 8:32

  And our success will come upon us like the flood from Heaven. Also, see the following verses of the Bible to guide you into the path of success which God has destined for the Man God Made.

- *If you confess with your mouth Jesus as Lord, and believe in your heart that God raised Him from the dead, you will be saved - Romans 10:9.*

- *For God so loved the world, that He gave His only begotten*

Son, that whoever believes in Him shall not perish, but have eternal life - John 3:16.

- *These things I have spoken to you, so that in Me you may have peace. In the world you have tribulation, but take courage; I have overcome the world - John 16:33.*

- *Do not store up for yourselves treasures on Earth, where moth and rust destroy, and where thieves break in and steal. But store up for yourselves treasures in Heaven, where neither moth nor rust destroys, and where thieves do not break in or steal; for where your treasure is, there your heart will be also - Matthew 6: 19-21.*

- *Delight yourself in the Lord and He shall give you the desires of your heart - Psalms 37:4.*

- *Therefore I say to you, whatever things you ask when you pray, believe that you receive them, and you will have them - Mark 11:24.*

- *If you abide in me and I abide in you, you shall ask what you desire and it shall be done unto you - John 15:7.*

- *This Book of the Law shall not depart from your mouth, but you shall meditate in it day and night, that you may observe to do according to all that is written in it. For then you will make your way prosperous, and then you will have good success - Joshua 1:8.*

- *In all your ways acknowledge God, and He will guide your paths - Proverbs 3:6.*

- *Commit your work to the Lord and your plans will be established - Proverbs 16:3.*

- *When a man's ways are pleasing to the Lord, He makes even his enemies to be at peace with him - Proverbs 16:7.*

- *He who is faithful in little will be faithful in much - Luke 16:10.*

- *For everyone to whom much is given, from him much will be required; and to whom much has been committed, of him they will ask the more - Luke 12:48.*

- *Be anxious for nothing but in all things by prayer and supplication with thanksgiving, let your requests be made known unto God and the peace of God which passes all understanding shall keep your heart and mind at peace through Christ Jesus - Philippians 4:6-7.*

- *The generous man will be prosperous, and he who waters will himself be watered - Proverbs 11:25.*

- *And my God will supply all your needs according to His riches in glory in Christ Jesus - Philippians 4:19.*

- *"Bring the whole tithe into the storehouse, so that there may be food in My house, and test Me now in this," says the Lord of hosts, "if I will not open for you the windows of Heaven and pour out for you a blessing until it overflows" - Malachi 3:10.*

- *Give, and it will be given to you. They will pour into your lap a good measure — pressed down, shaken together, and running over. For by your standard of measure it will be measured to you in return - Luke 6:38.*

- *Now this I say, he who sows sparingly will also reap sparingly, and he who sows bountifully will also reap bountifully. Each one must do just as he has purposed in his heart, not grudgingly or under compulsion, for God loves a cheerful giver - 2 Corinthians 9:6-7.*

- *But you shall remember the LORD your God, for it is He who is giving you power to make wealth, that He may confirm His covenant which He swore to your fathers, as it is this day - Deuteronomy 8:18.*

- *I will set no worthless thing before my eyes; I hate the work of those who fall away; it shall not fasten its grip on me - Psalms 101:3.*

- *But seek first His kingdom and His righteousness, and all these things will be added to you - Matthew 6:33.*

- *How blessed is the man who does not walk in the counsel of the wicked, nor stand in the path of sinners, nor sit in the seat of scoffers! But his delight is in the law of the LORD, and in His law he meditates day and night. He will be like a tree firmly planted by streams of water, which yields its fruit in its season and its leaf does not wither; and in whatever he does, he prospers - Psalm 1:1-3.*

- *By humility and the fear of the LORD are riches and honour and life - Proverbs 22:4.*

- *Ask, and it will be given to you; seek, and you will find; knock, and it will be opened to you. For everyone who asks receives, and he who seeks finds, and to him who knocks it will be opened – Matthew 7:7-8.*

As we leave this chapter, we should take the following wise sayings to heart:

The greatest among you shall be your servant. - Jesus Christ

Success is knowing your purpose in life, growing to reach your maximum potential, and sowing seeds that benefit others. - John C. Maxwell

Success is a journey, not a destination. - Anonymous

Behind every successful man there is a God-fearing woman. - Anonymous

I don't know the key to success, but the key to failure is trying to please everybody. - Bill Cosby

There are no secrets to success. It is the result of preparation, hard work, and learning from failure. - Colin Powell

Motivation Makes Mountain Movers Millionaires (The 5 Ms of Success). - Oghenethoja Umuteme

Finally, this is a word of encouragement taken from my book *How Good and Large Is Your Land?*

Move with the ball and drive with your heart. That's the rule of the game. Keep on moving. Dream your success. Work your success. Walk like a lion. Smile like an achiever. This is what it takes to move into your land of abundance.

CHAPTER FOURTEEN

MAN MADE FOR RESTORATION

I woke up at about 5am on the 9th of January 2012 with the words "and the word was made flesh" filling my heart. As I recited these words while waking up into the physical world, it dawned on me that this is all we need understand to enable us to reap the fruits of the restoration we have received in Christ Jesus.

Restoration of the Lost Man became possible when the "word became flesh" (John 1:14). This is that grain that had to become Earth in order to yield more grains. The spoken word must die and be buried in you first before the physical restoration can take place. We have to understand and digest every element of the spoken word, its physical form, and the wisdom to actualize its manifestation. When a living thing dies it has to be absorbed by the environment to enable its decay, and to be homogeneously mixed with the environment. And so the spoken word has to die, become buried, decay, and homogeneously absorbed into our hearts before it can bear fruit. So when God comes visiting us, He will see His spoken word taking the centre stage of our hearts (Jeremiah 17:9), where the word is absorbed and transformed into the Spirit of Christ (Galatians 4:6).

Restoration is only possible through a spoken word, and this can be seen in Isaiah 42:22 when God said: "...no one 'says' restore." The path to restoration is a path of light (Isaiah 42:16). And as we walk this path (Psalms 23:3), our hearts of stone, which are filled with unrepentant, unforgiving, unmerciful, sad, impure, etc thoughts, will gradually give way to a heart of flesh which is filled with "joy unspeakable."

A restored man is always in the presence of God, and in His presence there is fullness of joy; meaning that when we are in sorrow, we are out of His presence. The curse upon Adam and Eve would not have taken effect if they had not been cast out of the presence of God.

We are also told that Cain had to leave God's presence to serve his punishment. Anyone with the desire to be restored must ensure that any human act that will make God cast them out should be resisted. This is why we have to flee from every environment of sin. God started our restoration process with a spoken word, which must not return to Him without been manifested in our lives. He vowed, in Isaiah 42:16, to fulfil every word He spoke, which constituted the elements of His restoration game plan. The spoken word was filled with the fire of God; hence darkness could not comprehend it. To fully understand what we shall be gaining from God after being restored, we need to understand these words:

1. God with us (Isaiah 7:14, Matthew 1:23).
2. Those who believe shall never perish but they shall have eternal life (John 3:16).

To become fully restored, God spoke from Heaven Himself that we need to hear the word of restoration spoken by Jesus Christ: *this is my beloved son...hear Him (Mark 9:7).*

Saint Paul says that what we hear is called Faith. This means that Faith is that spoken word from God which had to take root in our hearts (Galatians 4:6), in order to turn it into a heart of flesh. So the process of restoration has a two-edged sword effect: removing satanic imperfections from our physical being, and piercing through our hearts to implant the love of God into us.

The Man God Made will have eternal life only when his spirit is redeemed. This is why Christ said it is only God that can destroy the spirit of man, which He came to redeem. This implies that a restored man experiences the joy of the Lord here on Earth first, and in Heaven eternal life. Our restoration, therefore, is in two stages. And we have to walk through the path of light to become restored. This light is the word of God (Psalms 119). You will never know what it takes to light someone else's candle until you are in the dark with a candle in your hands and looking for someone to help you with a matchbox to light it. The wisdom of God is the light of God. This is why the Bible says that Christ is the wisdom of God. People grope in the dark when they have no source of light with them. Not until God created light was the Earth filled with darkness. Even as we live, the only way to live here on Earth and experience the peace of God is when we are walking in His light (Isaiah 42:16). Those who don't have God grope in the dark, and anyone who gropes in the dark experiences stagnation in life.

God made me know that all I need to succeed is wisdom, and so, instead of struggling with the situations of life, I ask God for divine wisdom which will enable me to succeed, because of the wisdom I read in Ecclesiastes 10:10. Solomon asked for wisdom once and never returned to God again, hence he was led astray. We should make it a point of duty to always go back to God and ask Him for divine direction.

The spoken word has a spirit form which must take a physical form (flesh) to become useful to us. Once the spoken word proceeds from God, it has to be heard. Then what is heard has to fill our thoughts. This is to enable us to have the right physical imagination of what the spoken word is about to become. Once this is done, we are lifted out of our present state so that our desire to ensure that we achieve what we had seen in our mind will persist. This is when we ought to be closer to God so that the right wisdom is released to us in order to reduce our waiting period.

The waiting period is often filled with emotional instabilities, so the shorter the waiting period the better, to ensure we do not commit sin. If the Israelites had entered into the land of Canaan earlier, fewer people would have died. The longer the waiting period, the more pain we experience. Ecclesiastes 10:10 says that this period can be reduced through wisdom. And that wisdom is Jesus Christ!

To ensure that the word bears fruit in your life, the right imagination has to be resident in your heart, from where it will begin to cry out (Galatians 4:6), prompting you to take the right decisions, all the time. So, the word of restoration, once it is in our hearts, will take up the role of a supervisor, who ensures that the heart of the designer, which is replicated on a piece of paper, becomes a finished product.

God knew exactly what He expected to see when He said that the Man God Made will take His image and likeness. This means that anything devoid of that form is unacceptable to God. This is what the Spirit of God does in our lives. Your days must be fulfilled not in sorrow, but in joy. That is the role of the word in our lives. And this is the whole essence of FAITH. As a healing minister, and an oracle of God who says things to pass, the wisdom of God has to be resident in me. My son was ill some time ago and my wife came to lay him on my lap. I saw him restored to how he used to be when he was healthy, and he was healed instantly.

The Lord says in Nahum 2:2: *The LORD will restore the splendor of Jacob like the splendor of Israel, though destroyers have laid them waste and have ruined their vines.* The prophet knew exactly what God was going to restore. You cannot pray for things to pass when you don't have the right picture in your mind. To restore is to redeem. The Man God Made is one redeemed from the effect and the influence of sin (Galatians 4:4-6). For this to happen, we must be ready to seek the face of God. Jesus made Nicodemus to know this in John 3:3-5. This process includes the following stages:

- Born Again: Believing in Christ and confessing our sins.

- Born of Water: This involve the renewal of our mind leading to a feeling of true repentance within us. After undergoing this process, we will know when we are in sin, or when we are within a sinful environment. Our spirits become so active and informed.

- Born of Blood: The moment we are born of the blood, we start having the zeal for soul winning as the Spirit of Christ cries in our hearts (Galatians 4:6). This is when we begin to have human feelings, as Christ did. It is said that: "Blood is thicker than water." We will discover that we would find it difficult to be absent from the gathering of the brethren. We will not be comfortable until we partake in the Holy Communion. We begin to also see other believers as our own blood, because we are connected to one another through the blood of the Lamb. This is only when we can show love to one another through our acts.

It is only when we have gone through these stages that we can claim to have been saved and to be in the plan and purpose of God. In my book *The Path To Absolute Freedom*, I called these stages, "The Triple-I Model – Initiation, Intimation, Implantation." This is why the psalmist says in Psalms 54:1-2: *Save me, O God, by thy name, and judge me by thy strength. Hear my prayer, O God; give ear to the words of my mouth.*

Someone who is saved knows how to give to support the work of God. King David says in 1 Chronicles 29:14-17:

But who am I, and what is my people, that we should be able to offer so willingly after this sort? for all things come of thee, and of thine own have we given thee. For we are strangers before thee, and sojourners, as were all our fathers: our days on the Earth are as a shadow, and there is none abiding. O LORD our God, all this store that we have prepared to build thee an house for thine holy name cometh of thine hand, and is all thine own. I know also, my God, that thou triest the heart, and hast pleasure in uprightness. As for me, in the uprightness of mine heart I have willingly offered all these things: and now have I seen with joy thy people, which are present here, to offer willingly unto thee.

Who are we before God that we have to be begged before we can release ourselves for God's work? In the first place, the wealth that we have does not belong to us - we are only custodians. I have also seen greed ruling the hearts of men. Many would spend God's resources travelling round the world without a concern for the gospel. We shall account for all that God has kept under our care someday, as shown in the Parable of the Talents in Matthew 25:14-30. We are told in this portion of the Bible that the unprofitable servant will experience damnation:

And cast ye the unprofitable servant into outer darkness: there shall be weeping and gnashing of teeth.

Are you greedy towards the things of God? Mind you, if it is your responsibilities that are depriving you from serving God resourcefully, it was your own choice to marry (Proverbs 18:22) and give birth to the number of children you have, for instance. God didn't give Sarah, and even Rebecca, that many children. So don't expect God to overlook your nonchalant attitude towards His service because of the pains you are experiencing from your own desires. Someone who is redeemed values Heavenly things, but the unredeemed values material wealth, and makes much noise about it. Once we are redeemed, we ought to go out there to preach salvation unto others who are still unsaved. And, again, Job 8:5-7 says: *But if you will look to God and plead with the Almighty, if you are pure and upright, even now he will rouse himself on your behalf and restore you to your rightful place. Your beginnings will seem humble, so prosperous will your future be.- (NIV)*

We should learn to seek God's face before we sleep, if we are pure and upright, and He will lead us into the truth of life. This is where our quest for divine knowledge comes in. We must know when things are not right with us, and instead of pretending that all is well, we should enquire about our history, as espoused in the same Job 8: 8-10:

For enquire, I pray thee, of the former age, and prepare thyself to the search of their fathers: (For we are but of yesterday, and know nothing, because our days upon Earth are a shadow :) Shall not they teach thee, and tell thee, and utter words out of their heart?

If our days upon Earth are shadows, then we need to walk in the light of God for our shadows to show. Those who walk in darkness don't have shadows. To leave a mark on Earth, we need our shadows to be cast on Earth, which represents our good walk with God. We must enquire, in order to gather first-hand information about our ill situation. This points to the fact that the Man God Made is a researcher. You can also see more of this in my books, *Battles Beyond The Physical* and *The Path To Absolute Freedom*.

The process of restoration is the same as to tend. Jesus explained what this entails; it is not going to bring us physical comfort as many would think: And a certain scribe came, and said unto him, Master: *"I will follow thee whithersoever thou goest."* And Jesus saith unto him: *"The foxes have holes, and the birds of the air have nests; but the Son of man hath not where to lay his head."*

And another of his disciples said unto him: "Lord, suffer me first to go and bury my father."

But Jesus said unto him: "Follow me; and let the dead bury their dead." - Matthew 8:19-22

Adam was commanded to restore the garden daily to its intended original beauty. In Isaiah 42:22, God is saying that we are more interested in self-centred service rather than in the business of restoration. This perfect order was the only reason Christ came to die, so that we all could be restored in form, balance of reasoning and spiritual order. This is the only way we could become the image and likeness of God.

There came a time in Jesus' days when He had to curse all that He had blessed before, who had received healing because of their unrepentant heart (Matthew 11:21). We suffer because we have not made up our minds to repent. Several times I have been asked in the church during my teachings if there is anything like partial repentance. And I have told them time without number that repentance happens only once. The day we make up our mind to follow Jesus with no obligation attached to that decision, is the day we actually repented. But if our service to Him is aimed at some kinds of benefits, such as having a good job or a successful business, as many would do, then we would be thrown out of the path of salvation once we have challenges. Let's see Matthew 11:16-21 for what Jesus says:

16 But whereunto shall I liken this generation? It is like unto children sitting in the markets, and calling unto their fellows,

17 And saying, We have piped unto you, and ye have not danced; we have mourned unto you, and ye have not lamented.

18 For John came neither eating nor drinking, and they say, He hath a devil.

19 The Son of man came eating and drinking, and they say, Behold a man gluttonous, and a winebibber, a friend of publicans and sinners. But wisdom is justified of her children.

20 Then began he to upbraid the cities wherein most of his mighty works were done, because they repented not:

21 Woe unto thee, Chorazin! woe unto thee, Bethsaida! for if the mighty works, which were done in you, had been done in Tyre and Sidon, they would have repented long ago in sackcloth and ashes.

Our generation is no different from those referred to above. See verses 16 and 17: the children were sitting in the market place, mocking their fellows who were passing by, and going about their daily work, maybe rearing their father's flocks. There was no indication that they were actually playing any musical instrument, or if they were mourning, yet they claimed they were doing both. This can be confirmed from verses 18 and 19. And, because the people decided to sit in the market place as confirmed by their attitudes towards the gospel, mocking and not ready to change their attitudes, Jesus had to lay a curse upon them (verse 20, 21).

God made man in such a way that we could be restored. We are not perishable in nature, but renewable. This is the order of the spirit being - created for eternity. He gave man a heart that could adjust to situations, free will and the ability to become remorseful. He gave us eyes that could shed tears and ears that could hear counsel.

Man's rejection came at the summit of his admiration. The devil admired man's intelligence as he named all that have existed and anything that now exists. Today man still faces rejection by himself, the family, society and even God. Man's rejection has also led them to accept every kind of advice, from spiritualist to carnality, if only he could regain an inch of his lost glory.

I imagined man leaving the Garden of Eden that faithless evening. What was God thinking as He watched them depart His presence? Did He weep as Jesus did? Where did Adam think he was going? Did he ever imagine the obscured nature of the wild world he was taking his family into? Was he in his right senses, or was he under the influence of a sop (John 13:26)?

Why did both of them decide not to plead for forgiveness, rather than the blames they were laying? Adam lost his authority and influence over God's creation as he left that garden. As Adam and Eve took that sorrowful and painful step out of that Garden of God, so also their peace, opportunities, healthiness, fellowship with God and respect gave way, as the sun gives way to the moon at the eventide, to shame, disrespect, illness, disappointment, disfellowship and complaints. And the hallmark of that shame was the worship of idols - animals and trees, and images of both. Man became afraid of the world he was to restore and care for. Man started learning the means of survival from animals, and even sexual acts, after they were cast out of God's presence, that today we have people practising doggy sex position, dragon sex position, etc, as a means to having sexual satisfaction - What a shame! And, it would not be out of place to say that man learned sex from animals, because Adam only had sex with Eve after they left the Garden of Eden, into the field which was the habitat of animals, and so man became subjected to animal practices. Hence, early men were called barbarians.

The Bible passage below explains what God will do to anyone who cherishes self more than Him:

For, behold, the Lord, the Lord of hosts, doth take away from Jerusalem and from Judah the stay and the staff, the whole stay of bread, and the whole stay of water. The mighty man, and the man

*of war, the judge, and the prophet, and the prudent, and the ancient,
The captain of fifty, and the honourable man, and the counsellor,
and the cunning artificer, and the eloquent orator. And I will give
children to be their princes, and babes shall rule over them. And the
people shall be oppressed, everyone by another, and every one by his
neighbour: the child shall behave himself proudly against the ancient,
and the base against the honourable. - Isaiah 3:1-5*

If this is the case, then man needs restoration to become
who God made him to be. Restoration is both in the physical
and spiritual - authority, responsibility, defence, honour,
leadership, discipleship, orderliness, peaceful coexistence,
respect. People often think that to be restored means to
become wealthy overnight. Some will say St Paul says we can
do all things through Christ who strengthens us (Philippians
4:13), and as such they can do anything to make ends meet.
There is judgement ahead, if we care to know.

Restoration has to do with the renewal of the strength in
us. The Bible says that we can only achieve a fully restored
status through Christ that strengthens us; this means that you
can do something through Christ that strengthens you. Christ
is saying that if you abide in Him you shall bear more fruits
(John 15:5).

I read through the book of Nahum chapter 2 and verse 1
caught my fancy:

An attacker advances against you, Nineveh. Guard the

fortress, watch the road, brace yourselves, marshal all your strength! (NIV).

Even with all the warning and their preparedness, they were still defeated and enslaved. Why? Verse 7 says why: *It is decreed that Nineveh be exiled and carried away (NIV).*

This is the effect of sin. We may be experiencing what we are going through today because of the sin that lives in us. This is a hard truth that many would not want to hear. Pride has beheaded many of us, and we are fallen down like mere animals. In Obadiah 1:3-4, the Lord declares: *The pride of your heart has deceived you, you who live in the clefts of the rocks and make your home on the heights, you who say to yourself, 'Who can bring me down to the ground?' Though you soar like the eagle and make your nest among the stars, from there I will bring you down." (NIV).*

As a Christian, you cannot sell alcoholic drinks, for instance, or give them to somebody to drink. Alcohol negates the purpose of the Holy Spirit in us, because Saint Paul was saying in Ephesians 5:18 that it is good to be filled with the Holy Spirit rather than to be filled with wine. Restoration is about doing what is right all the time.

The first thing that should come into our hearts now is how we can be saved from all the curses upon us which we brought upon ourselves, due to our ignorance, negligence, iniquity, disobedience and every other manner of sin that we may have committed.

Even while the children of Israel were in Egypt as slaves, it was their desire that one day they should be delivered from the land of Egypt. Genesis 50: 22–26 gives us the scriptural story of what happened when Joseph was about to die:

And Joseph dwelt in Egypt, he, and his father's house: and Joseph lived an hundred and ten years. And Joseph saw Ephraim's children of the third generation: the children also of Machir the son on Manasseh were brought up on Joseph's knees. And Joseph said unto his brethren, I die: and God will surely visit you, and bring you out of this land unto the land which he sware to Abraham, to Isaac, and to Jacob. And Joseph took an oath of the children of Israel, saying, God will surely visit you, and ye shall carry up my bones from hence. So Joseph died, being an hundred and ten years old: and they embalmed him, and he was put in a coffin in Egypt.

This was Joseph's wish. Every man need restoration, but the fact remains that we must be ready and continually wishing for it to happen. I usually pray thus: God make me a salt that the world will desire all the days of my life. Gradually I could see this happening to me; we must keep on hoping and praying. It is better to wish yourself success in your prayers than wait for someone to do it for you. If you stop wishing yourself good, the devil will wish you evil. Any time you are praying, the devil only keeps quiet to hear what you are saying. And when you are silent, he will give you enough reasons why that prayer will not be answered. This is why we pray in the spirit, to destabilize the devil. Keep on praying in the spirit. Because it did not happen yesterday does not mean that it will not happen today.

And it shall come to pass in the last days, that the mountain of the Lord's house shall be established in the top of the mountains, and shall be exalted above the hills; and all nations shall flow unto it. And many people shall go and say, Come ye, and let us go up to the mountain of the Lord, to the house of the God of Jacob; and he will teach us of his ways, and we will walk in his paths: for out of Zion shall go forth the law, and the word of the Lord from Jerusalem. - Isaiah 2:2-3

When we walk into the path of God, all we need is to learn about Him and His ways. May the Lord be your peace, and may He take you through the journey that will make you the Man God Made.

CHAPTER FIFTEEN

SOCIO-SPIRITUAL DEHUMANIZATION

To dehumanize is to animalize. This is why I am not comfortable with the science of biology classifying humans as animals. This is what we have done to ourselves because of the social activities we indulge in. In an attempt to create worldly pleasures for ourselves, we have developed various pleasure items, such as sex toys, porn videos and magazines and the likes.

Plastic surgery to enhance beauty (including hip enhancement, facelifts etc), physique and sexual attractiveness such as breast enlargement, penile enlargement, vaginal enhancement, etc, are on the increase, with new techniques being invented daily. Sexy clothes, sexy hairdos, cat-walking, tattoos, etc, are the order of the day. Marriage is being redefined to include gay marriage. Virtual dating sites fill the internet, and now adultery is being committed virtually by the married.

I have seen men chatting with married women online, with the women naked and using webcams to show the men their sex organs. And then they will indulge in the act of masturbation. Sexual intercourse has been redefined to include oral sex, anal sex, in-between-breast sex, animal-human sex, phone sex, virtual-aided sex, etc, so that even married believers are now appreciating them and practising them, as they are being deceived by foolish ungodly pastors. We have also created brothels, club dance halls, ballrooms etc. Dances and various music genres are being develop to seduce the world into whoredom and idolatry.

In an attempt to associate, we have founded various occult groups, covens, idols, and so on. Knowledge is increasing, and instead of seeking after godly knowledge of comfort we have invented surrogate parenting, human cloning trials, in vivo and in vitro fertilization. Predominant now in Nigeria is the buying of children, which is different from adoption; and as such, we no longer wait on God to give us children the way He did to Abraham, Isaac, and Jacob. These acts have negated the essence of having faith in God in these homes.

Now we are suffering, and our prayers are not being answered. We have cried to God, to ask Him why He has kept deaf ears to our cries and God is replying:

Hast thou not procured this unto thyself, in that thou hast forsaken the LORD thy God, when he led thee by the way? - Jeremiah 2:17

Thy way and thy doings have procured these things unto thee;

this is thy wickedness, because it is bitter, because it reacheth unto thine heart. - Jeremiah 4:18

[You] have brought this upon you, because you lusted after the nations and defiled yourself with their idols. - Ezekiel 23:30 (NIV)

Because they have forsaken me, and have burned incense unto other gods, that they might provoke me to anger with all the works of their hands; therefore my wrath shall be poured out upon this place, and shall not be quenched. - 2 Chronicles 34:25

How long shall we keep on living in hypocrisy and apostasy? We can see our fault right there, in 2 Chronicles 34:25: "... that they might provoke me to anger with all the works of their hands." What are you crafting with your hands? The work of our hands is directly related to what we plant in our hearts, and then whom we revere. It is time we repented and stopped paying lip service to our dedication to God. Not until this is done are we part of this world, and we would end in that blazing fire of hell. Oral sex, anal sex, breast sex, watching porn movies, etc by married couples is sin. Avoid them if you are involved. Our dreams are becoming clouded, and we hardly know when the evil one is striking. We spend hours praying personal deliverance and spiritual warfare prayers, and less involvement in the act of soul winning, because we are still living in sin. People who claim faith in God carry olive oil about as anointing oil everywhere they go, without questioning themselves if the wisdom of God is in them first.

All those who left Egypt with Moses died in the wilderness because of their personal desires, not for the overall objective of obeying God. Even in the present day, many adults who just gave their lives to Christ still find it difficult to do the work of God because of their personal desires. This can also be seen in Matthew 19. When God called me, He said: "Go after the youths, and teach them what I reveal to you. The adults will only rebel against you, because they will see you as too young to tell them to repent."

I pray that the Lord accepts you, as you make a determined effort to walk with Him this day. Amen!

CHAPTER SIXTEEN

THE SEARCH CONTINUES

Let's look at this fact: God is looking for a son of peace, who will become an heir to His Kingdom. These are the ones who will inherit the Kingdom of God. They are those who are ready to fight the good fight of faith, here on Earth (1 Timothy 6:12).

These warriors are made up of individuals who have the qualities of the Man God Made. The first step, from what we have read so far, in becoming the Man God Made is having the spirit of selfless service. This involves us laying down our lives for the purpose of the gospel and tending the flocks of Christ. Many will argue that the flocks of Christ are those whom we refer to today as Christians. Christianity is not a religion, as many of us feel today; it is a body of faithful servants of God. The Church is made up of those who are called out of Egypt; the world of sin (Hosea 11:1), unto mount Zion, the Heavenly Jerusalem (Isaiah 30:19, Hebrews 12:22). Christianity is living in Christ-likeness, and being filled with the spirit of Christ (Galatians 4:6), through the continual renewal of our spirit being in Christ. These people make up the church of Christ worldwide. And they are present as individuals in every supposed House of God. Why did I use the term "supposed House of God?" The House of God is a home of unity, for those who are called out. What we have today is well explained in Revelation 17:15: *And he saith unto me, The waters which thou sawest, where the whore sitteth, are peoples, and multitudes, and nations, and tongues.*

This variance, which is also seen in the beliefs and attitudes of those we find in our present houses of God, will always breed murmuring, backbiting, pride and rebellion, leading to stagnation in our pursuit of spiritual growth and maturity. The church is made up of a chosen generation, who are peculiar and known for their Heavenly acts. They are royal priesthoods (1 Peter 2:9), and they are called as the priests of the Lord (Isaiah 61:6). They are the servants of the Lord (Revelation 7:3). And for the sake of these, God is not in a hurry to bring the world to an end yet, hoping that many more will embrace salvation and come to be with Christ in the new world that is to come: Saying, *Hurt not the Earth, neither the sea, nor the trees, till we have sealed the servants of our God in their foreheads. - Revelation 7:3*

The Man God Made is one who yields totally to the will of God, and must tell the people their sins so that they would repent. Gradually, instead of us having multitudes in our worship arenas, we would have the CHURCH worshiping God in the spirit (John 4:23-24), as in Acts 2.

This book has been in search for the qualities of these true worshippers of God, who are made up of the Man God Made. Revelation 14:2-5 are verses that will help us further in this search:

And I looked, and, lo, a Lamb stood on the mount Zion, and with him an hundred forty and four thousand, having his Father's name written in their foreheads.

And I heard a voice from Heaven, as the voice of many waters, and as the voice of a great thunder: and I heard the voice of harpers harping with their harps:

And they sung as it were a new song before the throne, and before the four beasts, and the elders: and no man could learn that song but the hundred and forty and four thousand, which were redeemed from the Earth.

These are they which were not defiled with women; for they are virgins. These are they which follow the Lamb whithersoever he goeth. These were redeemed from among men, being the firstfruits unto God and to the Lamb.

And in their mouth was found no guile: for they are without fault before the throne of God.

We are brought to the knowledge of the fact that the 144,000 who were redeemed from the Earth will be with Jesus wherever He would be, in thoughts and in their actions. They are the only ones who are gifted to sing and understand the new song of joy in Heaven. This is why I strongly believe that there are different languages in Heaven. The Angels, I believe, does not hear the conversation between God the father and Jesus, His only begotten son. This should be why we have Heavenly top secrets too (Deuteronomy 29:29).

This is what this book has presented: that the moment we become the Man God Made, everything around us will be perfect. And to understand secrets, God releases them to us in a pure language. From the Bible portion we just read, we can see the qualities of the Man God Made:

1. The intelligence to learn and understand spiritual interludes and codes (Revelation 14:3, Isaiah 42:16).

2. They are redeemed from the world, because there is no worldliness in them (Revelations 7:14, 14:3).

3. They are not defiled with women (Revelation 14:4). Many who argue that married people can have sex during church fasting and praying programs or before Sunday worship service should learn from this verse. If having sex with our wives is acceptable before Sunday services, why should the same God redeem only 144,000 to be with Jesus wherever He is (Revelation 14:4)? This may mean that the 144,000 are made up of mainly Catholic priests and popes, provided they meet up with the other requirements: *And in their*

mouth was found no guile: for they are without fault before the throne of God. Many of us have already missed the Heavenly Jerusalem, being among the 144,000 that would be with Jesus in mouth Zion. It could also refer to those who have not committed idolatry – see 1 Kings 19:18: *Yet I have left me seven thousand in Israel, all the knees which have not bowed unto Baal, and every mouth which hath not kissed him.*

But the usage in Revelation 14:4 clearly depicts purity from sexual intercourse. What do you think, especially when God is the one who instituted marriage?

4. They also suffer for the sake of the Gospel. If we do this, then we are only scrambling to be among the multitude referred to in Revelation 7:9, and these people also have a peculiar quality that made them acceptable unto God:
These are they which came out of great tribulation, and have washed their robes, and made them white in the blood of the Lamb. Therefore are they before the throne of God, and serve him day and night in his temple: and he that sitteth on the throne shall dwell among them.

Many of us belong to this last category, as long as we have already had sex, whether with our wives or someone else. But to merit being in the new Earth, we must also face opposition as preachers of the gospel. The multitude referred to above, which we are trying to be among, were living in sin, but they later accepted the gift of salvation by believing in Jesus, and doing His command (John 14:15-16).

In Matthew 5:1-11, Jesus let us know the kinds of people that make up a multitude:

And seeing the multitudes, he went up into a mountain: and when he was set, his disciples came unto him: And he opened his mouth, and taught them, saying,

Blessed are the poor in spirit: for theirs is the kingdom of Heaven.

Blessed are they that mourn: for they shall be comforted.

Blessed are the meek: for they shall inherit the Earth.

Blessed are they which do hunger and thirst after righteousness: for they shall be filled.

Blessed are the merciful: for they shall obtain mercy.

Blessed are the pure in heart: for they shall see God.

Blessed are the peacemakers: for they shall be called the children of God.

Blessed are they which are persecuted for righteousness' sake: for theirs is the kingdom of Heaven.

Blessed are ye, when men shall revile you, and persecute you, and shall say all manner of evil against you falsely, for my sake.

This is what makes up a multitude, and in the midst of these are those who will finally live the expected life that Christ taught them. Any time I remember the vision I had of those sentenced to everlasting doom in that courtroom, I get scared for this generation. This portion of the Bible defines the expected attitudes (eg hunger and thirst after righteousness) and duties (eg comfort those that mourn) of the Man God Made. This is only when that multitude referred to in Matthew 5:1-11 is saved from the great tribulation. To this end, we would agree that we must have the heart of God to live on Earth and thereafter become saved by Him in the end. Revelation 14:6-7 says:

And I saw another angel fly in the midst of Heaven, having the everlasting gospel to preach unto them that dwell on the Earth, and to every nation, and kindred, and tongue, and people, Saying with a loud voice, Fear God, and give glory to him; for the hour of his judgment is come: and worship him that made Heaven, and Earth, and the sea, and the fountains of waters.

This is what we must do; acting like the Angel in the Bible portion above, and preaching the good news to our generation so that they are not cast into the winepress of the wrath of God (Revelations 14:19).

Goodbye.

EPILOGUE

God needs you – every part of you, because you are bought with the blood of Jesus (1 Corinthians 6:20). This is why your body is His temple. A temple is the housing for the Altar and those who officiate at the Altar.

God is more interested in His work than the pleasures of life we are having today. Many of us will obey our husbands, wives and bosses more than God. Heaven is made for those who lived for God. I have searched through the Bible and I have seen that over time, when God chooses men to do His will, He is more concerned about the fruits men bear in His name, while He takes responsibility for how their families fare. But funnily enough, the care of our families is the reason why many of us have decided to abandon the work of God. We find it difficult to follow up new souls because we are mindful of what people will say, especially when they are of the opposite sex. We have belittled ourselves to the extent that unbelievers are now the ones who control our lives with their tongues. Pastors find it difficult to minister privately to female souls as Jesus did to the Samaritan woman by the well. When the disciples came and saw Jesus with the woman, they marvelled at that scene, because it wasn't normally done:

And upon this came his disciples, and marvelled that he talked with the woman: yet no man said, What seekest thou? or, Why talkest thou with her? - John 4: 27

It was like a taboo, and today many of us have also allowed this to continue in our era, therefore denying Christ so many souls we would have won to Him. We do this because we still allow our pasts to play a role in our new-found faith of love and care. And this points to the fact that we are still thinking evil:

Brethren, be not children in understanding: howbeit in malice be ye children, but in understanding be men. - 1 Corinthians 14:20

If a man can see a pastor for counselling in secret like Nicodemus did, why can't a woman also see her pastor in secret? After all, men could also seduce the pastor, to have anal sex with him. Why am I arguing this? It is because the Man God Made was a perfect man in thoughts. And even while Adam and Eve lived in that garden alone, they never had sexual intercourse until they departed from the garden; which is to say that a man and a woman can stay together alone without necessarily being involved in sexual intercourse.

Once we can refine our thinking about sex, we will become free to win all manner of souls to Christ. Inasmuch as the Samaritan woman and "the woman caught in the very act", both of whom could be said to be prostitutes, got the attention of Jesus Christ, we ought to go out there and save our society from the snare of prostitution. It is my proposal that churches should build hostels to house prostitutes and lead them to Christ, in order to train them in ministry work. Many of them could become evangelists, for instance (Galatians 4:1-2). The church could also train them in skills for their upkeep.

I might want to care for a sister, for instance, bringing her close to me so that she will feel loved and cared for, but the world frowns at it, and people may come attacking, the way the disciples felt the world should have done to Jesus, in John 4:27. A pastor is supposed to be close to the widows in the church, but will the world see him as innocent? A woman in need can go to any lengths to see that she gets attention, as the woman with the issue of blood did, and we must be aware of this fact. Instead of pushing them away as cheap sex hawks, we should have the wisdom to counsel them, and provide long-lasting solutions to their ailment by ensuring that they are indoctrinated in the faith. This needs a lot from the male, whom they often feel free to relate their issues to.

One day Ruth's mother-in-law Naomi said to her, "My daughter, I must find a home for you, where you will be well provided for. Now Boaz, with whose women you have worked, is a relative of ours. Tonight he will be winnowing barley on the threshing floor. Wash, put on perfume, and get dressed in your best clothes. Then go down to the threshing floor, but don't let him know you are there until he has finished eating and drinking. When he lies down, note the place where he is lying. Then go and uncover his feet and lie down. He will tell you what to do." - Ruth 3:1-4 (NIV)

The last statement there points to the reason for her going secretly to meet Boaz: "He will tell you what to do." And this is the act of counselling. Now see her request in verse 9: "I am your servant Ruth," she said. "Spread the corner of your garment over me, since you are a guardian-redeemer of our family."

This statement of hers did not mean in context that Boaz should marry her, but help her become a settled woman. Now Boaz talks of Ruth's integrity (verse 10-11):

You have not run after the younger men, whether rich or poor. And now, my daughter, don't be afraid. I will do for you all you ask. All the people of my town know that you are a woman of noble character.

This means he knew much about her. How many pastors know much about the ladies, and the widows in their midst? Something more happened, after he had made her stay with him through the night, in verse 14:

So she lay at his feet until morning, but got up before anyone could be recognized; and he said, "No one must know that a woman came to the threshing floor."

Does this negate the fact that Ruth actually slept there through the night? No! But Boaz was trying to please the people's conscience and evil thoughts. Are we to do the same? And Boaz went to the extent of given himself as the solution to the woman's quest. Jesus gave His life for us. Did Mary alone not go down to seek Jesus at the tomb? (John 20:1). Did that make the disciples see her as one dating Jesus before His crucifixion? Even when I have a revelation concerning a sister, I have to ensure I don't call her on phone to tell her, because someone may feel I am dating her. Our thoughts must be refined, for the purpose of the Kingdom of God.

Those who have the reasoning of the Kingdom of God don't think of their sex, because there is neither male nor female in God's Kingdom. We are all one and the same. God created them, male and female; let's stop this discrimination and go out to win souls of all kinds. Hannah the widow prophetess stayed all her life in the temple of God, ministering before God, in the midst of the priests (Luke 2:36-38). If it were now, many of us would say it is not acceptable for a woman to minister before God, and we would be thinking she was having an affair with the priests. Sins have clouded our reasoning. Our discrimination acts have rendered the women weaker by the day, and the children they bring forth are becoming weakened too without the word of God in them. Women can become pastors and ministers in God's house, and they can extend this act into their homes, to raise a God-fearing society and a church for God.

Soul-winning requires selflessness. In Matthew 19:12 Jesus opened up this fact of those seeking the Kingdom of God:

There be eunuchs, which have made themselves eunuchs for the kingdom of Heaven's sake. He that is able to receive it, let him receive it.

People becoming eunuchs for the sake of God's Kingdom shows the level of sacrifice God is requesting from us. There are many families today who bother so much about their own pleasure while God is looking for labourers. I have seen many who would rather spend the resources God has given to them in travelling around the world with their families to satisfy their curiosity, not in the furtherance of the gospel of Christ, and seeing Satan fall (Luke 10:18), but come back and tell stories of how beautiful the lands they visited are, and they would want to go back again as the Israelites wished to go back to Egypt (Exodus 14:12). Jesus explained to us what it meant to be the Man God Made in our service of dedication to God:

While he yet talked to the people, behold, his mother and his brethren stood without, desiring to speak with him. Then one said unto him, Behold, thy mother and thy brethren stand without, desiring to speak with thee. But he answered and said unto him that told him, Who is my mother? and who are my brethren? And he stretched forth his hand toward his disciples, and said, Behold my mother and my brethren! - Matthew 12: 46-49.

If our immediate family is more important to us than the work of God, then we are living in hypocrisy. Anyone who finds it hard to support God's work and paying their vows is still being invaded by the wicked (Nahum 1:15). How many of us have Apple IPods and IPads for our children when the next door neighbour's child's school fees are yet to be paid? God spoke to me in a dream one night: if you want increase, there is a man living there (He pointed at the compound), and his son's school fees are not paid yet. I quickly responded, and I can see God's increase in my life. Abraham denied his wife because he was more concerned about the vision he was championing for God, and God restored her back to him. Moses' father-in-law had to bring his wife and children to him in the wilderness. Jesus made us know that we have a lot to leave before we can follow him (Mark 10:29, Matthew 19:21).

The devil uses what we give attention to to derail us. We have given too much attention to sexual relationships, so that even now, many would practise pornography in the name of marriage covenant in their homes. Marriage is now more about sex, without giving time for God. Many would say that St Paul talks of both consenting to the fact that they must avoid sex for the sake of God, and as such the man or woman would have no choice to stay out of sex, waiting on the Lord (1 Corinthians 7:5).

How does this measure up with Jesus' statement in Matthew 19:12? This means that if one's spouse does not have time for the things of God, the other too should avoid God. Paul was a eunuch, and was Heaven conscious. His advice was only human, for a generation who were self conscious only, because those he ministered to were still in the world. But he believes that as they receive faith continually, they will begin to give less attention to the flesh, and desire the things of God more.

Let me give this illustration: Someone you ignore will always try to catch your attention until you attend to them. This is how the devil works. You have renounced him in public, and he wants to tell people that you are still his friend by coming close to you. If you give him your attention, he will quickly let the world know that you haven't followed Christ. Will Christ bother about what the world says He is? He only bothered about who Peter said He was, and the testimony of God the father revealed severally of Him.

Christ never discriminated between a female and a male. The man sat at Jesus' feet on one occasion (Luke 8:35), and on another occasion Mary sat at His feet (Luke 10:39). It is a popular saying that: "what's sauce for the goose is sauce for the gander." Not until we give attention to the female sex, ensuring that women are matured in wisdom and in spiritual matters, will they keep on raising children without godly intent, and the purpose of the Man God Made will never be realised.

COVENANT CONFESSION

If you are not born again, you may have read this book like a literary material and will not receive the spirit it carries. You can make a decision to correct that now by saying this covenant confession.

Lord Jesus, I know now that you died for my sins. I believe and confess you as my Lord and Saviour. Please come into my life and dwell inside of me.

If you just said this confession, you should locate a spirit filled church to fellowship with them – let the pastor know you just gave your life to Christ and you will be directed on what to do next. Salvation is a personal race and you must be serious with it.

You can also give us a call through the numbers below:
+234-8076190064; +234-8086737791.
Or send us email at:
christmovementinternational@gmail.com

BOOKS BY THE SAME AUTHOR

Existing In The Supernatural
The Altar In Golgotha
How Good and Large is your Land?
Born To Blossom
Battles Beyond The Physical
The Path To Absolute Freedom
The Man God Made

To contact Pastor Oghenethoja Umuteme send an email to
president@christmovementinternational.org

You can join him on Facebook and Twitter also:
www.facebook.com/Pst Oghenethoja Umuteme
www.twitter.com/PstUmuteme

WORSHIP WITH US
@
ROYAL DIAMONDS INT'L CHURCH
(aka Christ Movement)
Nnata Close by Weli Street
Rumunduru/Eneka Road
Rumunduru
Port Harcourt, Nigeria

Please call or send us email to know our
worship days and time.
Phone: +234-8086737791

Email: christmovementinternational@gmail.com
info@christmovementinternational.org

NOTES

NOTES

NOTES

www.ingramcontent.com/pod-product-compliance
Lightning Source LLC
LaVergne TN
LVHW051625080426
835511LV00016B/2183